D1770010

The Story of Gotama Buddha

Pali Text Society

The Story of Gotama Buddha

The Nidāna-kathā of the Jātakaṭṭhakathā

Translated by

N.A. Jayawickrama

Published by
The Pali Text Society
Bristol
2011

First published	1990
Reprinted with corrections	2000
Reprinted	2011

© Pali Text Society 1990

ISBN-10 0 86013 293 5
ISBN-13 978 0 86013 293 6

Printed in Great Britain by
CPI Antony Rowe Chippenham

CONTENTS

Preface ix

Translator's Original Introduction xiii

Preamble 1

The Three Epochs 2

The Distant Epoch 3

The Story of Sumedha 3
The Path Leading to Nibbāna 5
Renunciation as an Ascetic 7
The Power of Insight 8
The Buddha Dīpaṅkara 14
Resolution to Gain Enlightenment 17
The Eight Conditions 18
The Buddha Named Gotama 19
The Portents 21
The Contributory Conditions to Enlightenment:
The Perfection of Generosity 25
The Perfection of Morality 25
The Perfection of Renunciation 26
The Perfection of Wisdom 27
The Perfection of Effort 27
The Perfection of Patience 28
The Perfection of Truth 29
The Perfection of Resolution 29
The Perfection of Amity 30
The Perfection of Equanimity 31
The Perfections 31
The Buddha Named Gotama 32
Songs of Praise 33

The Assurances 35
Dīpaṅkara 35
Koṇḍañña 38
Vijitāvī 38
Maṅgala 38
The *Yakkha* Kharadāṭhika 39
Suruci 40
Sumana: Atula 44
Revata: Atideva 45
Sobhita: Ajita 45
Anomadassi: The *Yakkha* General 46

Paduma: The Lion 46
Nārada: The Ascetic 47
Padumuttara: Jaṭila 47
Sumedha: Uttara 48
Sujāta: The Universal Monarch 49
Piyadassī: Kassapa 49
Atthadassī: Susīma 50
Dhammadassī: Sakka 50
Siddhattha: Maṅgala 51
Tissa: Sujāta 51
Phussa: Vijitāvī 52
Vipassī: Atula 53
Sikhī: Arindama 53
Vessabhū: Sudassana 54
Kakusandha: Khema 54
Koṇāgamana: Pabbata 55
Kassapa: Jotipāla 56
The Buddhas 56
The Perfection of Generosity 57
The Perfection of Morality 58
The Perfection of Renunciation 59
The Perfection of Wisdom 59
The Perfection of Effort 60
The Perfection of Patience 60
The Perfection of Truth 60
The Perfection of Resolution 60
The Perfection of Amity 61
The Perfection of Equanimity 61

The Intermediate Epoch 63
The Threefold Uproar 63
The Invitation of the Deities 64
The Five Great Considerations:
(i) The Time 64
(ii) The Country 65
(iii) The Family 65
(iv) The Mother 66
(v) Her Life Span 66
Conception of the Great Being 66
Queen Māyā's Dream 66
The Soothsayers 67
The Thirty-Two Omens 67
The Bodhisatta's Mother 69
Her Journey to Devadaha:
The Branch of the Sāla Tree 69
The Four Great Brahmās 70
The Two Streams of Water 70

The Seven Strides 70
Mahosadha 71
The Seven Sahajātas 71
Kāḷadevala 71
He Receives His Father's Homage 72
The Child Nālaka 73
The Interpreters of the Marks 74
The Group of Five 75
The Four Omens 76
The Ploughing Festival 76
The King Pays Homage a Second Time 77
The Bodhisatta Displays His Skill in the Arts 77
The Four Omens 78
The Bodhisatta is Adorned 80
Rāhula's Birth 81
Kisāgotamī 81
The Dancing Girls 82
The Great Renunciation 82
Rāhula 83
Kanthaka 83
Māra 84
The River Anomā 85
The Shrine of the Crest Gem 86
The Requisites of a Monk 87
Kanthaka 87
Visit to Rājagaha 87
Austerities 89
Sujātā 90
The Bodhisatta at the Foot of the Tree 91
The Golden Bowl 92
The Bowl Goes Upstream 93
The Grass-Seller Named Sotthiya 93
The Seat of Enlightenment 94
Māra's Legions 95
The Deities Flee 95
The Battle with Māra 96
The Earth as Witness 98
Māra's Defeat 98
The Proclamation of Victory 98
The Great Being Gains Omniscience 99
The World in Festive Array 100
The Ecstatic Utterance 100

The Recent Epoch 103
The Seven Weeks:
The First Week 103
The Shrine of the Steadfast Gaze 103

The Shrine of the Jewelled Cloister 103
The Shrine of the House of Gems 103
Māra's Sixteen Lines 104
The Daughters of Māra 105
Mucalinda 106
Tapassu and Bhalluka 107
Brahmā's Solicitation 108
His Journey to Bārāṇasī 108
The Pañcavaggiyas 109
The Proclamation of the Wheel of the Dhamma 109
The Clansman Yasa 110
The Bhaddavaggiyas 110
The Three Brothers, Matted-hair Ascetics 111
King Bimbisāra 111
Sakka 113
The Acceptance of Veḷuvana 114
Sāriputta and Moggallāna 114
King Suddhodana Wishes to See His Son 115
Kāḷudāyī 115
The Blessed One Visits Kapilavatthu 117
Kāḷudāyī Receives Alms at Kapilavatthu 117
The Blessed One Performs a Miracle 118
The Sākiyas Pay Homage to the Blessed One 119
The Blessed One Begs Alms in the City 120
Rāhula's Mother Pays Homage 122
Nanda 123
Rāhula 123
Rāhula's Ordination 123
The King's Attainment of the Fruits of the Non-Returner Stage 124
Anāthapiṇḍika 124
The Acceptance of Jetavana 125
In Praise of the Dedication of Monasteries 126
Jetavana as the Residence of all Buddhas 126

Index 129

PREFACE

The text translated here is the Nidānakathā, literally "the story of the origins" (or "antecedents"), which is extant as an introduction to the collection of stories of the past lives of the Buddha Gotama, the Jātaka,[1] which forms part of the fifth and last part of the Sutta-piṭaka, the Khuddaka Nikāya. Like those stories, it contains three different kinds of text: first there are verses, which are perhaps the oldest layer of the text; secondly, there is a prose elaboration and explanation of the verses; and third there is a word-commentary (here found on only three occasions). Both the prose elaboration of the verses and the word-commentary are generally thought by modern scholarship to have been written by the same author; traditionally this is said to have been the great fifth-century scholar-monk Buddhaghosa. The prose elaboration sometimes simply repeats what the verses say, with barely any additional information; sometimes the verses would be unintelligible without the long sections of prose connecting them. The prose elaboration and word-commentary together are called Jātakatthavaṇṇanā, "Jātaka commentary". In the edition of the text published by Fausbøll, the word-commentary is printed in smaller type, and we have followed that convention in this translation.

The text falls into three parts:

(i) The first, after a brief preamble, is the "Distant Epoch" (*Dūre Nidāna*). This itself contains two sections: first, the story of how Siddhattha Gotama, in a previous life as the ascetic Sumedha, made the vow to become a Buddha himself, rather than join Dīpaṅkara's Buddhist community (*saṅgha*) as a monk and attain *nirvāṇa* there and then, followed by a list of the ten Perfections which must be fulfilled on the path to Buddhahood; and second, an account of the previous Buddhas who prophesied the future Buddhahood of Gotama, with brief sketches of the form in which Sumedha/Gotama was reborn on each

[1]For a fuller account, see K.R. Norman, *Pāli Literature* (Harrassowitz, Wiesbaden, 1983), pp. 77–84, 128–29; and M. Winternitz, *A History of Indian Literature* (rev. ed. Motilal Banarsidass, 1983), pp. 108–51, 180–83.

occasion, followed again by the list of Perfections, this time with references to Jātaka stories which exemplify each one.

(ii) The second, the "Intermediate Epoch" (*Avidūre Nidāna*), takes the story from the time of the future Buddha's (the Bodhisatta's) descent from the Tusita heaven and birth as Siddhattha Gotama to the attainment of Enlightenment (here called "Omniscience", *sabbaññutā*, as commonly in later literature).

(iii) The third, the "Recent Epoch" (*Santike Nidāna*), deals with the Buddha's temptation by Māra and his daughters, his decision to preach, and various events in the early days of his teaching, up until the donation of the Jetavana monastery by the great lay-follower Anāthapiṇḍika.

This text, like all works of Buddhaghosa and other Pali commentators, was not written *de novo*, but consciously drew on previous works, Canonical and commentarial, in both Pali and Sinhalese. It declares its dependence on two other works in the Khuddaka Nikāya, the Buddhavaṃsa, and the Cariyāpiṭaka (although the version of the Cariyāpiṭaka used was clearly different from that now extant); it also refers to other texts of the Canon, ascribes opinions to other commentaries and teachers and to "members of the School of Abhidhamma". The story of Siddhattha's seeing the "Four Omens" and subsequent Renunciation follows a similar story told of a previous Buddha, Vipassī, found in the Mahāpadāna Sutta of the Dīgha-nikāya, to which the text refers; the third and last section, the "Recent Epoch" (*Santike Nidāna*) is clearly dependent on the account of the early days of the Buddha's teaching found now in the Mahāvagga of the Vinaya-piṭaka. Many other incidents in the story are also found scattered throughout the Canon. Although biographical and on occasion autobiographical stories of the Buddha's life are found in these and other texts, the Nidānakathā is the first large-scale connected biography of the Buddha Gotama found in Pali; it is not, however, complete, but stops with the donation of the Jetavana monastery, and ends with an encomium on the advantages of donating monasteries. The inclusion in texts of passages explaining such advantages (*ānisaṃsā*) occurs in the earliest literature, and was to become very widespread, both in Pāli and in the vernacular languages of Theravāda countries.

The Nidānakathā has been translated before. T.W. Rhys Davids' early version was made in 1880 and published as *Buddhist Birth Stories*.[1] Like all his translations it is elegant and generally accurate, but there are some errors, and his style is now rather archaic; this is particularly the case with his use of Christian terminology ("gospel" for *dhammadesanā*, "angel" for *deva*, etc.). He did not translate the word-commentary. H. Warren's *Buddhism in Translations*, first published in 1896, contains a rendering of parts of the *Dūre Nidāna* and all of the *Avidūre Nidāna*; for the *Santike Nidāna* he substituted the Vinaya account. The version presented here is therefore the only complete translation of the Jātakatthavaṇṇanā text, and the only one made in this century. It was first published in Sri Lanka in 1951, together with an edition of the Pāli text in Sinhalese characters. The present version contains a number of changes and additions to the translation and notes, all of which have either been made or approved by Professor Jayawickrama; we have included his original Introduction, and the titles for different sections of the story which he had inserted. Numbers in square brackets refer to the text edited by Fausbøll and published by the PTS; occasionally different readings are recorded in the footnotes.

We publish *The Story of Gotama Buddha* as part of the Pali Text Society's paperback series, for use in universities and colleges, and by the general reader.

August 1989 Steven Collins

[1]Rhys Davids' original intention was to translate the entire Jātaka collection, as is seen in this title; the first editions of this work contained versions of most of the first forty Jātaka stories as well as his translation of the Nidāna-kathā. But he abandoned the plan, and all of the Jātakas were subsequently translated by E. Cowell *et al.* Rhys Davids' version of the Nidāna-kathā was then republished alone, with some emendations by C.A.F. Rhys Davids, under the same title.

THE TRANSLATOR'S ORIGINAL INTRODUCTION

The Nidānakathā of the Jātakaṭṭhakathā serves as an introduction to the text of the Jātakas contained in that work. In spite of the fact that it is meant as a preface to the Jātakas, however, it bears all the characteristics of an independent work. Under the three divisions Dūre, Avidūre, and Santike Nidāna, it deals with the story of the Buddha from his existence as Sumedha up to the acceptance of the monastery of Jetavana. The Dūre Nidāna consists of two parts: one, the Story of Sumedha; and the other, the Assurances he received under twenty-four Buddhas. The discussion of the Pāramitās occupies an important place in the narrative. The Avidūre Nidāna narrates the incidents from the Bodhisatta's departure from Tusita up to his attainment of Enlightenment. The Santike Nidāna purports to give "the numerous instances which make reference to his stay at various places", but stops short with Buddha's visit to Sāvatthi where Anāthapiṇḍika built for him the Jetavana monastery. This story itself has little bearing on the "Birth Stories commencing with Apaṇṇaka, which that great and illustrious sage, had narrated of yore"; and the Nidānakathā makes only passing reference to a few Jātakas which any other work posterior to the latter would have done. On the other hand, the fact that it deals with the Bodhisatta's career is deemed sufficient reason to make this introductory story preface the collection of Jātakas. Besides, the occasional references to the Nidānakathā in the "current episodes" (*paccuppannavatthu*) of some of the Jātakas may strengthen the claims of the Nidānakathā as being an essential part of the Jātakaṭṭhakathā, provided the authenticity of these *paccuppannavatthus* can be established.

The problems connected with the Nidānakathā are vastly different from those associated with the Jātaka. In so far as they affect the Nidānakathā they have to be touched upon here. Sinhalese and Burmese tradition is strong in attributing the Jātakaṭṭhakathā to the great commentator Buddhaghosa. He is said to have translated into Pāli the Jātaka stories that were found in Sinhalese. The greater probability is that this tradition conveys only an incomplete picture of the actual event in an attempt to attribute this work to Buddhaghosa. This voluminous work cannot possibly be indebted to this source alone (Sīhalaṭṭhakathā), for leaving aside the Porāṇā whose tradition was authoritative in most matters, there is bound to have existed a nucleus of a Jātaka collection prior to its crystallization in the present form. No doubts can be cast on the early existence of the Jātaka verses which are included in the Khuddaka Nikāya as its tenth book. The oral traditions connected with these Jātaka verses, which by themselves are unintelligible, contained most of the tales now incorporated in the Jātakaṭṭhakathā. It is not improbable that all these Jātakas were compiled together by one editor who supplied the commentary and in some cases filled in gaps where necessary. In addition to these, there is a large number of Jātakas preserved in the Suttas of the Pāli Canon: e.g. Mahāsudassana Sutta, Mahāgovinda Sutta, Makhādeva Sutta, etc. But there is little or no conclusive evidence to suggest that we owe all this to Buddhaghosa. As noted by Rhys Davids (*Buddhist Birth Stories*, p. lxiii foll.) and Burlingame (*Buddhist Legends*, H.O.S. Vol. 28), the commentaries to the Jātaka and Dhammapada differ considerably from Buddhaghosa's commentaries, in point of language and style; and Winternitz (*History of Indian Literature*, Vol. II, 192) concludes that he cannot possibly have written them. All that can be said is that a compiler in Sri Lanka, probably in the commentarial epoch, revised the extant Jātaka tales, translating the available material in Sinhalese, at the same time making free use of other commentaries as may be seen from instances such as: "The statement made in the Jātaka Commentary that at that time Prince Rāhula was seven days old is not found in the other commentaries", as stated in our text. What applies to the Jātakaṭṭhakathā holds good with the Nidānakathā as well.

The Nidānakathā is the earliest attempt in Pāli to give a connected life-story of the Buddha. Works like the introductory chapter of Vinaya Mahāvagga, the Buddhavaṃsa, and Cariyāpiṭaka have preceded it. But they have not taken up a connected narrative of the life of the Buddha. Many of the incidents mentioned in the biographical account in the Vinaya are summarised in the Santike Nidāna, while the Dūre Nidāna is greatly indebted to the Buddhavaṃsa and Cariyāpiṭaka, and in fact, includes the whole of the second chapter of the Buddhavaṃsa. At frequent intervals it makes quotations of stanzas from these two works. In its description of the Ten Perfections, the Nidānakathā borrows a great deal from the Cariyāpiṭaka. But the differences shown in the two works with regard to the details have led scholars like Charpentier (*WZKM*, 1910, 351 foll.) to conclude that the present Cariyāpiṭaka is a re-arrangement of an earlier recension and that the Nidānakathā has based its description of the Pāramitās on the latter. Several incidents mentioned in the Nidānakathā are reported in isolated suttas in earlier Canonical works. Events connected with the Great Renunciation are seen to occur in the Mahāpadāna Sutta of the Dīgha-nikāya, and the Nidānakathā refers to it by name. The Mahāpadāna refers to six other Buddhas who are also mentioned in the Nidānakathā, while it deals fully with the story of the Buddha Vipassī. Several Suttas of the Majjhima-nikāya, viz. Mahāsīhanāda, Mahāsaccaka, Bodhirājakumāra, Saṅgārava, and Ariyapariyesana, contain a full account of the Renunciation and striving, though stripped of all the embellishments found in the Nidānakathā. The noble quest (*kiṃkusalagavesana*) is an important factor in the above suttas though the Nidānakathā dismisses it with a few lines. However, the treatment of the six years of struggle cannot be called inadequate, though the above suttas from the Majjhima give minute details not found in our work. The account of the miracles at the birth of the Bodhisatta is for the most part based on the Acchariyadhamma Sutta of the Majjhima Nikāya, while the Bhayabherava Sutta, also of the Majjhima, contains an account of the Buddha's attainment of Enlightenment, which is repeated in many other suttas of the Dīgha- and Majjhima-nikāyas, e.g. Dvedhāvitakka Sutta. The encounters with Māra are found in isolated passages of the Saṃyutta- and Khuddaka-nikāyas. Three early poems dealing respectively with the birth, renunciation, and striving of the Bodhisatta are found in the Sutta-nipāta (Nālaka, Pabbajjā, and Padhāna Suttas), and the Nidānakathā refers the reader to the Pabbajjā Sutta and its commentary when it describes the Bodhisatta's first meeting with Bimbisāra, king of Magadha. The Māgandiya Sutta gives the Buddha's account of his abandoning his life of pleasure in the three palaces. The events narrated in the Santike Nidāna more or less follow the account in the Vinaya Mahāvagga, though not in such great detail. As a work of the same period, the Buddhavaṃsa-aṭṭhakathā also furnishes some information found repeated in the Nidānakathā.

The Nidānakathā does not stand alone as a work of its class. Later writers like Buddharakkhita, the author of Jinālaṅkāra (1156 C.E.), and Vanaratana Medhaṅkara, the author of Jinacarita (in the latter half of the 13th Century C.E.) wrote ornate poems on the life of the Buddha, while the Mālālaṅkāra-vatthu, a biography of the Buddha, was written in Burma (1773 C.E.). On the other hand, Buddhist Sanskrit works belonging to a period earlier than the Nidānakathā offer closer parallels to it, though they are voluminous works as compared with it. The Mahāvastu, which is also called the Vinaya of the Lokottaravādins of the Mahāsāṅghika School, contains a biography of the Buddha which generally agrees with the account in the Nidānakathā. The only claim of the Mahāvastu to be the Vinaya is that it contains a few facts dealing with admission to the Order, found in the earlier chapters of the Pāli Vinaya Mahāvagga. Besides this, the biographical details found in Mahāvagga I are seen to occur in the third book of the Mahāvastu. This corresponds to the Santike Nidāna of the Nidānakathā. The other two books of the Mahāvastu contain sections parallel to the Dūre and Avidūre Nidānas of the Nidānakathā. The extraneous matter embodied in Mahāvastu makes it difficult to sort out a connected story, and therefore the importance of the similarities between the two works is thereby diminished. The Lalitavistara which is considered as a Mahāyāna work, starting from its second chapter, gives a biography of the Buddha. It begins where the Avidūre Nidāna commences in the Pāli version. The exceedingly close agreement with early Pāli accounts has led scholars to believe that "the Lalitavistara is a recast of an older Hīnayāna text, the Buddha-biography of the Sarvāstivāda School, enlarged and embellished in the spirit of Mahāyāna" (Winternitz, II, 252). The book contains divergent strata which are not clearly separable into their various layers. Last but not the least, should be mentioned the great epic Buddhacarita of Aśvaghoṣa, the greatest of all Buddhist poets.

Although these Buddhist Sanskrit works are anterior to the Nidānakathā, the tradition preserved in them, the phase of development in ideology, and their conception of the Buddha represent a stage of growth subsequent to that portrayed in the Nidānakathā, which is more faithful to the original Pāli tradition of the earlier Nikāyas, while it has absorbed some of the principles of Mahāyāna seen to occur already in works like the Buddhavaṃsa and Cariyāpiṭaka. The Pāramitās are recognized, but there is no reference to the ten Bhūmīs which find mention even in a work like the Mahāvastu, a book that marks the transition from early Buddhism to Mahāyāna. The docetic tendency prevalent among the Lokottaravādins, as seen from the Mahāvastu, cannot be traced in the Nidānakathā, for it is the Bodhisatta who is born to this world and not the Buddha. This aspect is greatly accentuated in the Lalitavistara where Buddha's appearance on earth is termed an "act of sport" (*lalita*), and he is exalted as a divine being. In spite of the frequent introduction of miracles and the supernatural, quite often authenticated in earlier works, the human character of the historical Buddha stands out pre-eminent. He is undoubtedly exalted, but that comes as a result of his omniscience and Enlightenment. He is superior to all devas and men but is not a divinity who resides in Sukhāvatī. The doctrines of the Tathāgatagarbha and Trikāya are foreign to the Nidānakathā. Thus, it is abundantly clear that the Nidānakathā, taken as a whole, is earlier than these Buddhist Sanskrit works in contents and character, though chronologically it was written after them.

It is not proposed to discuss here problems connected with the Jātakas which have been dwelt on at length by scholars. I refer the reader to the following works: V. Fausbøll's edition of the Jātaka text in six volumes with an index (Vol. VII) by Dines Andersen; Ven. Widurupola Piyatissa's edition of the text in the Simon Hewavitarne Bequest Series; *Buddhist Birth Stories*, consisting of a translation of the Nidānakathā and Jātakas 1–40, by T.W. Rhys Davids; *Jātaka Tales*, a translation of selected Jātakas by H.T. Francis and E.J. Thomas; the translation of the Jātakas under the editorship of E.B. Cowell (six volumes and an index volume), T.W. Rhys Davids' *Buddhist India*; W. Geiger's *Pali Literature and Language*; B.C. Law's *A History of Pali Literature*; M. Winternitz's *A History of Indian Literature*, Vol. II; and *Encyclopædia of Religion and Ethics* (aricle on Jātaka), R. Fick: *Social Organization*.

The following books may be consulted in addition to them in studying the Nidānakathā: *Cambridge History of India*, Vol. 1 (the relevant chapters); E.H. Brewster's *Life of Gotama the Buddha*; E.J. Thomas's *The Life of the Buddha as Legend and History*; Rockhill's *Life of Buddha*; Kern's *Der Buddhismus* I, which contains a free rendering of the contents of the Nidānakathā; Warren's *Buddhism in Translations* containing the translation of the Dūre and Avidūre Nidānas.

The present edition of the Nidānakathā is meant for the general reader to become acquainted with the traditional story of the life of the Buddha. The earlier translations mentioned above are not easily available while the best known of them, *Buddhist Birth Stories*, has been long out of print. I have ventured to suggest interpretations to certain passages which have been either left untranslated or translated differently by Rhys Davids. The translation includes the commentarial passages which have been dismissed as unnecessary, and an attempt is made to render faithfully the Pāli as far as possible. As such, this translation may be of some use to the student as well.

January 1951 N.A.J.

THE NIDĀNAKATHĀ OF THE JĀTAKAṬṬHAKATHĀ

ADORATION TO HIM, BLESSED, WORTHY AND ALL-ENLIGHTENED!

1.[1] The great Sage, the leader of the world who has accomplished beyond measure the welfare of the people during many thousands of crores[2] of births,

2. Making obeisance at his feet, paying homage to the Doctrine and showing reverence to the Brotherhood, the receptacle of all honour,

3. And surmounting all obstacles by the efficacy of that meritorious act consisting of paying homage to the Three Gems,

4. The Birth Stories commencing with Apaṇṇaka, which that great and illustrious Sage, being faced with diverse circumstances had narrated of yore,

5. In which the Teacher, the Leader [of the world], being bent on the salvation of mankind, brought into maturity over long, the vast constituents for Enlightenment,

6. And whatever was rehearsed together under the name of Jātaka by those who made the recension of the Scriptures making a compilation by collecting all of them together,

7. I, who have been requested by the Elder Atthadassī, who came to me with his desire for the perpetuation of this chronicle of the Buddha,

---

[1] Abbreviations: A = Aṅguttara-nikāya, Bv = Buddavaṃsa, D = Dīgha-nikāya, Dhp = Dhammapada, *DPPN* = *Dictionary of Pāli Proper Names* (G.P. Malalasekera), Fsb = Fausbøll's edition of the Jātaka (Pali Text Society), MW = Monier-Williams' *Sanskrit–English Dictionary*, *PED* = *Pali–English Dictionary*, S = Saṃyutta-nikāya, SHB = Simon Hewavitarne Bequest Series edition in Sinhalese script, Sn = Suttanipāta, Sp = Samantapāsādikā (commentary on the Vinaya), Th = Theragāthā, Vin = Vinaya-pitāka.

[2] A crore (Pāli *koṭi*) = 10,000,000.

8. And who leads a life detached from the world, always in the company of his fellow monks, and likewise by the wise Buddhamitta of tranquil mind,
9. Adept in methodical exposition and sprung in the lineage of Mahiṃsāsaka; and further by Buddhadeva the monk of keen intellect,
10. The Commentary to the Jātaka which illustrates the glory of the deeds of Great Beings which is beyond imagination,
11. Will expound, closely associating myself with the method of exposition current among the dwellers of the Great Monastery. May the virtuous retain it well in mind while I speak![1] [**2**]

The Three Epochs

This commentary on the Jātaka, if it be expounded laying down the Three Periods, the Distant Epoch, the Intermediate Epoch, and the Recent Epoch, will be clearly understood by those who listen to it, since they will have followed it from the very beginning; therefore we shall expound it laying down the three periods.

Herein, from the very outset, should the limits of those periods be understood. The continuous narrative from the time of the resolution made by the Great Being at the feet of the Buddha Dīpaṅkara up to his birth in Tusita heaven after passing away from his existence as Vessantara, is called the Distant Epoch. The continuous narrative from the time he passed away from Tusita heaven up to his attainment of Omniscience at the throne of Enlightenment [at the foot of the Bodhi-tree], is called the Intermediate Epoch. And the Recent Epoch is to be seen in the various places he frequented on his sojourns far and wide. Here follows the Distant Epoch.

---

[1] These eleven stanzas are all a single sentence, each stanza has been translated separately: the subject is "I" (verse 7), the verb is '"will expound" (verse 11), and the object "the Commentary to the Jātaka" (verse 10).

THE DISTANT EPOCH

(Dūre Nidāna)

THE STORY OF SUMEDHA

Four *asaṅkheyyas*[1] and a hundred thousand æons ago, there was once a city called Amaravatī. Here lived a brahmin called Sumedha, of noble birth on both sides, maternal and paternal, of pure descent[2] for seven generations, unimpeached, and not held in reproof in point of birth, handsome, pleasing to behold, amiable, and endowed with an excellent complexion and beauty. Engaging in no other work he acquired brahmanical lore alone. While he was still in his youth his parents died. Then the official in charge of his wealth brought the accounts book, and opening the rooms filled with gold, silver, jewels, pearls, and other precious things, declared "Prince, so much belonged to your mother, so much to your father, and so much to your grandparents and great-grandparents"; and pointing out the wealth owned up to the seventh generation past asked him to make use of it. The Wise Sumedha reflected: "My parents, grandparents, and others who had amassed this wealth did not take with them even a *kahāpaṇa*[3] when they left this world; but I should so act as to take it along with me." With the king's permission[4] he sent out proclamation by beat of drum in the city, and giving away his wealth in charity to the common people he renounced the world for the sake of the ascetic life. In order to make the full significance of this statement explicit, the story of Sumedha should be narrated here. Even though it occurs in full in the Buddhavaṃsa,[5] on account of the fact that it is handed down in metrical form, it is not quite

---

[1]Lit. "a period beyond all reckoning." The duration of a *kappa* (an æon) may be imagined from the similes in Pali texts, but an *asaṅkheyya* is so vast a period that it cannot be known by anyone.

[2]*Gahaṇika* chiefly refers to the purity of the mother who gives birth to a *kula-putta* so described in this phrase, *gahaṇi*, lit. womb.

[3]A small copper coin.

[4]Lit. "having told the king about it."

[5]Bv Chapter II foll.

clear. Therefore we shall narrate it with frequent statements explaining the stanzas.

Four *asaṅkheyyas* and a hundred thousand æons ago there was a city named as Amaravatī or Amara, always resounding with the tenfold city-din, concerning which it is said in the Buddhavaṃsa, **[3]**

12. Four *asaṅkheyyas* and a hundred thousand æons ago there was a city named Amara, pleasant and delightful, not bereft of the ten sounds, and abounding in food and drink.

Here "not bereft of the ten sounds" means that it was not free of these ten sounds: the sound of elephants, of horses, of chariots, of drums, of kettle-drums, of lutes, of song, of conch-shells, of instrumental music, and that of "eat, drink, and be merry" as the tenth. Describing one aspect only of these sounds the stanza,

13. The trumpeting of elephants, the neighing of horses, the sounds of drums and conches, the din of chariots and the cries of "eat and drink" with the invitation to partake of food and drink

is found in the Buddhavaṃsa; and next it proceeds:

14. The city [was] replete with all the required constituents, full of all pleasures, possessing the seven precious things, thronged with diverse peoples, the abode of virtuous men and as prosperous as the city of the devas.[1]
15. There was in the city of Amaravatī a brahmin named Sumedha, the owner of a fortune worth many crores, possessing much wealth and grain.
16. He was learned in the Vedas,[2] knowing the mantras[3] by heart, having attained perfection in the three Vedas and reached mastery in prognostication, in traditional lore, and in the discharge of his duties.

---

[1]This word is normally translated as "deities" though often devas are loosely referred to as gods. The word is derived from the root *dyu* "to shine" (cp. Pali verb *jotati*).

[2]The sacred texts of the brahmins, originally three in number (Ṛg, Yajur, and Sāma) with a fourth (Atharva) added subsequently.

[3]Hymns of the Vedas, primarily of the Ṛg Veda.

The Path Leading to Nibbāna

Then one day, the Wise Sumedha was remaining in solitude in the splendid upper storey of his mansion, and began to reflect seated cross-legged: "O wise man, painful indeed is conception in a new existence, so is the dissolution of the body in whatever place one is born. And I am subject to birth, decay, disease, and death. Being such as I am, it behoves me to seek for the great immortal state of Nibbāna, which is tranquil and free from birth, decay, disease, and both pain and pleasure. Surely there must be a unique path that leads to Nibbāna, affording release from becoming." Accordingly it is said:

17. Seated in seclusion, I then thought thus: "Painful is rebirth and the dissolution of the body.
18. "I am subject to birth, decay, and disease. Then do I seek that calm refuge free from decay and death.
19. "Let me discard this putrid body filled with all things that are foul and depart hence with no yearning and desire for it. [4]
20. "There is and there will be such a path, for it cannot but be. I will seek that path to win perfect release from becoming."

He further thought "Just as there is, in this world, pleasure which is diametrically opposed to pain, so where there is becoming there must be its opposite, non-becoming: and just as when there is heat there is also cold, so there must be Nibbāna that extinguishes the fires of lust and the like; and just as there is the noble and blameless condition which is diametrically opposed to the evil and ignoble state, so where there is the evil of birth, there must be Nibbāna, designated as birth-free, as it brings birth to destruction." For it is said:

21. Just as where there is pain there is pleasure, so where there is becoming non-becoming is to be desired.
22. Just as where there is heat there is cold, so where there is the three-fold fire[1] Nibbāna is to be expected.
23. Just as where there is evil there is also good, so where there is birth non-birth is also implied.

---

[1]The fires of lust, ill-will, and delusion.

He further reflected, "Just as a man who has sunk in a heap of filth, having seen from afar a large lake covered with the five kinds of lotuses, should seek that lake thinking 'what is the path that would lead me there?' — and if he does not seek it, it is not the fault of the lake — so, when there is the great lake of the deathless Nibbāna which washes away the stains of defilement, its not being sought is not the fault of the great lake of the immortal state of Nibbāna. And if a man who is surrounded by robbers does not escape when there is present a means of escape, the fault is not in the means but in the man himself. In the same way, where there is the blessed road leading to Nibbāna for the man who is encompassed and overwhelmed by defilements, its not being sought after is not the fault of the road, but that of the man himself. And if a man who is afflicted with a disease does not seek the aid of a physician who is at hand and capable of treating his ailment, and does not get his disease cured, it is not the fault of the physician. Likewise, if he who is oppressed with the disease of defilements does not seek the Teacher who is at hand and who is proficient in the path leading to the allaying of defilements, the fault lies with him and not with the Teacher who makes an end of defilements." Therefore it is said:

24. Just as when a man who has fallen into filth, having seen a lake full to the brim, does not seek it, it is not the fault of the lake;
25. So when there is present the lake of immortality that washes away the stain of defilements, if one seeks it not, it is not the fault of the lake of immortality. **[5]**
26. Just as when a man who is set upon by enemies does not flee, although there is a way of escape, it is not the fault of the road;
27. So, when there is the blessed path, if one beset with defilements does not seek it, it is not the fault of the good path.
28. Just as when a man who suffers from an ailment does not get himself treated for that disease when there is a physician at hand, it is not the fault of the physician;
29. So, if a man who is oppressed and tormented by the diseases of defilements does not seek that Teacher, it is not the fault of that spiritual guide.

He further reflected "Just as a man who is accustomed to be gaily clad goes in comfort throwing away a carcass suspended on his neck, even so should I, with no attachment for it, discard this putrid body and enter the city of Nibbāna. And as men and women discharging their excrement on the depositing ground do not take it with them in their laps or wrapped in the folds of their garments, but depart discarding it with loathing, with no desire for it whatever, even so should I discard this putrid body with no attachment for it and enter the city of Nibbāna. And as sailors go away abandoning without any attachment for it a ship that is falling apart, even so will I discard without any attachment for it this body which oozes with matter from its nine festering apertures and enter the city of Nibbāna. And just as a man who carries with him many precious things going along the same road with some robbers, takes a safe road avoiding them for fear of losing his jewels, in like manner this foul body is comparable to a jewel-plundering robber; and if I form any craving for it, the precious gem of the Good Teaching leading to the noble path will be lost to me; therefore it behoves me to abandon this body which is like unto a robber and enter the city of Nibbāna." Therefore it is said:

30. Just as a man goes in comfort and freedom with full control over himself having with revulsion freed himself from a carcass tied to his neck;
31. So will I forsake this foul body, a heap of putrefaction, and go away with no attachment and yearning for it.
32. Just as men and women discharge their fæces in the depositing ground and go with no attachment and yearning for it;
33. So will I go forsaking this body which is full of all things foul, as one leaves the privy having discharged waste matter.
34. Just as the owners forsake a crumbling craft, broken and water-logged, and go with no attachment and yearning for it; [**6**]
35. So will I forsake this body with its nine apertures and constant outflow of matter, as the owners have forsaken the frail craft.
36. Just as a man who carries goods with him, parts company with robbers if he is travelling with them, for fear of losing his goods;
37. So will I go, forsaking this body, which is like a mighty robber, for fear of harm coming upon my virtue.

Renunciation as an Ascetic

The Wise Sumedha, having thus, with diverse similes, reflected on this subject which is associated with renunciation gave away [as aforesaid] his unlimited accumulated wealth to beggars and wandering mendicants in charity at his residence; giving up material and sensual pleasures he left the city of Amara for the Himalayas where he built for himself a hermitage in the vicinity of the peak called Dhammaka and made a hut and a cloister which were free from the five defects. And in order to evolve the power called higher knowledge, which is accompanied by eight justifiable qualities, often described with such statements as "when the mind has attained such composure", in that hermitage he renounced the world as an ascetic, discarding his mantle with its nine disadvantages and donning a bark garment possessing the twelve advantages. Having thus become a religious mendicant he gave up his hut which had its eight disadvantages and resorted to the foot of a tree with its ten advantages, and sustained himself on fruits that came his way, rejecting all preparations made of grain. Being engaged in the practice of severe austerities in his bodily postures of sitting, standing, and pacing up and down, within a week he gained mastery of the eight attainments and the five forms of higher knowledge. He thus attained the powers of higher knowledge in accordance with his resolution. Therefore it is said:

38. Having thus reflected, I gave my wealth worth many hundreds of crores to the rich and the poor alike and repaired to the Himalayas.
39. Not far from the Snowy Mountain is the peak called Dhammaka. There I built with care and diligence my hermitage and hut.
40. There I built a cloister, devoid of the five defects and possessed of the eight attendant advantages; and I evolved the powers of insight.
41. Then I discarded my raiment, with its ninefold faults, and wore a bark-made robe with its twelve attendant virtues.
42. I forsook my hut beset as it was with eight shortcomings and drew near the foot of a tree possessed of its ten advnatages.
43. Without exception I rejected all grain, both sown and grown, and gathered for food the fallen fruits with their many wholesome ways. [7]
44. There I strove with exertion in sitting, standing, and pacing, and within a week attained the strength of higher wisdom.

The Power of Insight

In this text it is stated that the hermitage, hut and cloister were built by the Wise Sumedha himself. But here follows its meaning: Sakka the lord of the devas who beheld the Great Being as he set out with the intention of penetrating into the Himalayan region and reaching the peak Dhammaka on the same day, addressed the *devaputta*[1] Vissakamma: "Go, dear friend; the Wise Sumedha over yonder has set out thinking of renunciation. Build for him a dwelling place." He agreed to carry out his request and created a delightful hermitage, a well sheltered hut, and a beautiful cloister. And the Blessed One has said with reference to that hermitage which appeared as a result of the potency of his merit, "O Sariputta, on that peak Dhammaka,

"I built with care and diligence my hermitage and hut; there I built a cloister devoid of the five defects."

Herein "I built with care" means "built carefully by me"; "the well erected hut" means that even the house with its thatch of leaves was erected carefully. "Devoid of the five defects" signifies the five defects enumerated as: hardness and unnevenness, trees growing inside it, being covered with weeds, being too confined, and being too extensive. One who walks on a cloister built on hard and uneven ground hurts one's feet, and blisters appear on them, the mind gains no tranquillity, and the topic of meditation becomes obscure; but by walking comfortably on soft and even ground the exercises in meditation bring results. Therefore hardness and unevennness of the ground should be considered as one of the drawbacks. If there is a tree standing within the cloister, whether in the centre or towards the end, one would strike one's forehead or head on it as one paces up and down without paying attention to it. This is the second disadvantage, the presence of a tree within it. One who walks on a cloister overgrown with grass and creepers treads on creatures such as serpents in the dark, and either kills them or suffers much pain by being bitten by them. This is the third disadvantage, its being overgrown with weeds. One who paces in a too confined cloister, a cubit[2] or half a cubit in length, stumbles on its boundary and injures the toenails or the toes. This is the fourth disadvantage, its being too confined. One who paces in a too extensive cloister allows the mind to wander and is unable to concentrate. This is the fifth disadvantage, its being too extensive. A cloister one and a half cubits in width, with a side-walk of a bare cubit on either side, and sixty cubits in length, with a soft surface evenly strewn

[1]*Devaputta* also means "deity". When the character of a deity is definitely masculine the terms *deva* and *devaputta* are used in preference to *devatā* which is grammatically in the feminine gender.

[2]*Ratana*, a linear measure (see *PED* s.v. *ratana*[2]). In the Sinhalese tradition current even today 2 *vidatthi* (spans) = 1 *ratana* and is the length from elbow to the tip of the middle finger. Cp. also Vedic *aratni* (see s.v. in MW), in Vedic times an *aratni* was reckoned from the elbow to the tip of the little finger. The table is: 12 *aṅguli* = 2 *vidatthi* = 1 *ratana*, 7 *ratana* = 1 *yaṭṭhi*, and 12 *yaṭṭhi* = 1 *usabha*.

with sand is most suitable. The cloister of the Elder Dipappasadaka Mahinda[1] of Cetiyagiri was one like that. Therefore it is said, "I built a cloister there, devoid of the five defects." The statement "endowed with the eight good qualities" means that it was possessed of the eight advantages accruing to a monk. The following are the eight advantages: the absence of possessions such as wealth and grain; the necessity for going in quest of alms which is blameless; eating food thus begged with perfect composure; security from the tyranny of ruling clans over their territories when they collect as tithes their share in stable property and money consisting of lead and copper coins; absence of any attachment or liking to objects of everyday use; absence of the fear of being robbed by thieves; absence of intercourse with kings and ministers of state; and the absence of obstruction from the four quarters. [**8**] And so it is said "I built there a hermitage endowed with the eight good qualities, because by living in that hermitage it is possible to benefit from these eight advantages accruing to a monk." The statement "I evolved the powers of higher wisdom" means "Later, while living in that hermitage, having performed the preliminary exercises for the *kasiṇa*[2] meditation and gaining introspective knowledge by reflecting on impermanence and sorrow for the evolution of the powers of higher knowledge and of the attainments, I gained the consolidated powers of introspection". The significance is: "Since I am able to gain that power, living there, I have built that hermitage making it suitable for the gaining of higher knowledge and the powers of intuitive wisdom".

Here follows the story giving the context of the statement "I discarded my garment with its nine faults". It is said that the *devaputta* Vissakamma returned to the deva world having created a hermitage equipped with hut, rock cell, cloister, and so forth, hidden behind many flower and fruit-bearing trees, containing a delightful reservoir of refreshing water, protected from wild beasts and dangerous birds and suited for a life of seclusion, having provided a reclining board at either end of the beautiful cloister and placed a green stone-slab with an even surface at the centre of the cloister for sitting on, and provided inside the hut, all the requisites of a hermit such as a skullcap for the matted locks, a bark garment, a trident, a crooked staff; and water pitchers, shells, and cups for drinking water in the outhouse; coal pans, firewood, and other articles in the kitchen; having created everything that is of use to a hermit and inscribed on a wall of the hermitage the words: "Those who wish to renounce the world may do so using these requisites"; [then] the Wise Sumedha, while he was

[1]Lit. "he who has infused serene joy in the Island". This is a reference to the Elder Mahinda, Emperor Asoka's son, who established Buddhism in Sri Lanka.

[2]*Kasiṇa*, the aids to *kammaṭṭhāna* or topics of meditation enumerated as *paṭhavi* (earth) *āpo* (water), etc. (See Visuddhimagga.) The word is etymologically connected with *kasiṇa* (Sk. *kṛtsna*) meaning "entirety" or "whole". Phrases such as *paṭhavi-kasiṇa* are sometimes translated as "earth-artifice", etc., but there is no apparent justification for such a translation.

looking for a comfortable place for his lodging, following the course of the mountain cascades on the foothills of the Himalayas, saw at the river's bend this delightful hermitage, Sakka's gift, the creation of Vissakamma, and walked up to the end of the cloister where he failed to see footprints. Thinking that the recluses living in it were most likely to be seated inside the hut being tired after their return from begging their food in the alms village, he waited a short while, and wishing to find out the cause of their delay, opened the door of the cell of the hermitage and entered within. While he was looking around the place he read the inscription on the main wall, and decided that those requisites were suitable for his use and that he should take them and renounce the world. He then discarded both his inner and outer garments. Accordingly it is said "There I discarded my garment"; "O Sariputta, having thus gone inside I discarded my garment with its nine disadvantages, in that hermitage" means "I discarded my garment seeing its nine disadvantages". These are the nine disadvantages arising from garments to recluses who renounce the world as ascetics: their being very costly is one disadvantage, having to depend on others to obtain them is another, and their becoming soiled quickly by use is another. When a garment becomes soiled it has to be washed and dyed. Its wearing away by use is another disadvantage. When it has worn out and become threadbare it has to be strengthened by padding it up. The difficulty in obtaining it even by going in search of one is a further disadvantage. Its incompatibility with the ascetic life is another. Another disadvantage is that it can be held in common even with thieves, for it has to be looked after so that they will not steal it. A further disadvantage is that it forms an adornment to the wearer. And the other is that it becomes a burden on one's shoulders and arouses great attachment to it. The meaning of the statement "I donned the bark garment" is "O Sariputta, then I saw these nine advantages and discarded my garment and donned the bark garment. **[9]** I took for my inner and outer garments the bark raiment made of shreds of muñja[1] grass woven together". "Possessing the twelve virtues" means that it was endowed with the twelve advantages. There are twelve advantages arising from a bark garment: first, it is of little value, pleasant and permissible for use; second, it can be woven by oneself; third, it does not become soiled easily by use and it does not take long to wash; fourth, it can be mended when it is worn out by use; fifth, it can be made easily when the need for a new one arises; sixth, it is suitable for the ascetic life; seventh, it is of no use to thieves; eighth, it forms no adormnent to the wearer; ninth, it is very light wear; tenth, it brings about contentment as regards robes; eleventh, the material for the garment can be obtained by righteous and lawful means; twelfth, even if the bark garment is lost it causes no regret.

[1]A kind of grass (reed) sacred to the brahmins and used at sacrifices.

How did I give it up when it is said, "I forsook my hut beset with eight shortcomings"? Taking off my pair of costly garments I took the red bark garment resembling a garland of *anoja*[1] flowers from the bamboo robe hanger where it lay hanging and put it on, wearing above it another bark garment of golden colour, and placed on one shoulder a deerskin with hooves, which resembled a spread of *punnaga*[2] flowers. I untied the skullcap for the matted locks and placed a pin made of hard wood in the topknot in order to make it firm. I next untied the coral coloured water pot from the suspension cord which resembled a string of pearls, and taking the *pingo* pole which was bent at three places, I suspended at one end the water pot, and at the other the hook and basket and the trident. Placing on my shoulder the shoulder yoke, I took the ascetics' staff in the right hand and left the hut. Pacing up and down the extensive cloister of sixty cubits I looked at my new guise and was encouraged with such considerations as "My ambition is fulfilled! My renunciation is perfect! The ascetic life has indeed been praised and extolled by all the great heroes such as the Buddhas! I have destroyed the fetter of household life! I have gone forth in renunciation! I have received the highest ordination! I will fulfil the duties of a monk and attain the bliss of the fruits of the Path!" I laid aside the burden on my shoulders and spent the rest of the day seated motionless like a golden statue on the green stone slab placed in the centre of the cloister. At eventide I entered the hut and relaxed my limbs lying down on the spread of rushes on the bedstead made of split bamboos; and rising at early dawn I reflected on my arrival there: "I have seen the evils of household life and entered the forest, forsaking unlimited wealth and unending glory. I have become a religious mendicant in my quest for renunciation. From now on it behoves me not to be remiss in my duties. Perverse reflections, like flies, devour him who wanders about forsaking solitude. Now I deem it fit to foster my seclusion. As for me, I have gone forth seeing that the household life is beset with obstacles; and this is a pleasant hermitage, its plastered floor is of the colour of the ripe *bilva*[3] fruit, its white walls are radiant as silver, the thatch of leaves is of the colour of a dove's foot, the bamboo bedstead is of the colour of a beautiful carpet, the dwelling place has all the comforts of a house, and it appears to me that there are no comforts which a household can offer besides these." Reflecting in this manner on the disadvantages of the hermitage he saw eight. The following are the eight disadvantages arising from the use of a hermitage: the first is the necessity for exerting oneself in doing various work connected with putting together the numerous articles which belong to it; **[10]** the second is the need for constant vigilance in replacing again and again the straw, leaves, and plaster when they are dislodged from where they are; preference in the occupation of dwellings should be given according to seniority, and when one is awkened at unusual hours one is not able to attain tranquillity of mind — being thus subject to being awakened at any time is the

[1]A shrub with red flowers used for making wreaths.

[2]A tree noted for its sweet smelling flowers. Sinhalese *domba*.

[3]The Aegle fruit. Sinhalese *beli*.

third disadvantage; the sensitiveness [of the body] caused by being sheltered from the cold and heat is the fourth; the fifth is that it conceals all censurable acts, for a person who remains within closed doors can commit any evil deed; looking upon it as personal property is the sixth; the very fact of the presence of a house necessitates its being shared by other inmates — this is the seventh; the eighth is that it forms a common possession, as it is equally well shared by lice, bugs, house lizards, and other creatures. Seeing these eight disadvantages the Great Being gave up the hermitage. Therefore it is said: "I abandoned the hermitage which was beset with eight disadvantages." The meaning of "I repaired to the foot of a tree possessed of its ten advantages" is explained as "Having discarded the concealment within, I went to the foot of a tree which was endowed with its ten advantages". Thereof, the following are the ten advantages: first, it necessitates little activity; second, it requires little tending, for one has only to walk up to it; third, it requires no attention as it can be conveniently used, whether swept or not; fourth, it provides no cover for a censurable act, for it conceals no misdeed, and one shrinks from committing an evil deed there; fifth, it causes physical hardiness, for there is nothing like the open-air life that brings about physical hardiness; sixth, it is not held as a possession; seventh, it dispels the attachment for a house; eighth, unlike in a house shared by many, there is no necessity to be requested to leave with words to the effect, "I am about to tidy it up, please leave"; ninth, it brings joy to the person who leads this life; and tenth, as the shelter of the foot of a tree is found in abundance wherever one goes, there is no cause for anxiety. It is said that "I resorted to the foot of a tree seeing these ten virtues". Pondering over all these matters, the Great Being set out for alms on the following day. Thereupon, the people of the village he visited gave him alms with much enthusiasm. Having finished his meal he returned to the hermitage, and seated himself, reflecting, "It is not with the idea of obtaining food that I have become a mendicant friar, but this soft food increases my intoxicating pride and sexual virility. There is no limit to the misery arising from food. Let me give up all food derived from grain, both sown and grown, and subsist on the fruits that come my way." Thenceforth he acted in that manner and striving hard, full of endeavour, he evolved within a week the eight attainments and the fivefold intuitive knowledge. For it is said:[1]

> Without exception, I rejected all grain, both sown and grown, and gathered for food fallen fruits with their many wholesome ways.
>
> Then I strove with exertion in sitting, standing, and pacing, and within a week attained the strength of higher wisdom.

[1]Above, p. 8, vv. 43, 44.

The Buddha Dīpaṅkara

While the ascetic Sumedha was thus passing his days in the bliss of the attainments, having reached the strength of intuitive knowledge, the Teacher called Dīpaṅkara appeared in this world. At the time of his conception, his birth, his Enlightenment, his setting a-roll the wheel of the Dhamma, the entire ten thousand world systems [11] quaked and trembled, shuddered, and created a mighty din. The thirty-two portents manifested themselves. The ascetic Sumedha, who was passing his days in the bliss of the attainments, neither heard that sound nor beheld those portents. For it is said:

45. While I had thus attained the peak of my attainments and gained mastery in the ascetic order, the Conqueror named Dīpaṅkara, the Leader of the world appeared.
46. Being devoted to the bliss of the ecstatic [*jhāna*-]meditation,[1] I did not see the four omens, at his conception, his birth, his Enlightenment, and his preaching of the doctrine.

At this time, the Buddha Dīpaṅkara of ten powers while on his wanderings in due succession, accompanied by four hundred thousand arahants,[2] reached the city of Rammaka and took up his residence in the great monastery Sudassana. The citizens of Ramma heard that Dīpaṅkara, the foremost among monks who had reached the highest Enlightenment and had set rolling the noble wheel of the Dhamma, had taken up his residence in the great monastery Sudassana on arriving at the city of Ramma on his sojourns from place to place; they took with them medicaments such as clarified and fresh butter, cloth and raiment, and went to the Teacher carrying incense, garlands, and other gifts in their hands, being greatly attracted by, inclined towards, and drawn greatly towards the Buddha, the Dhamma, and the Brotherhood. They worshipped him, made offerings of perfumes and the like, and sitting down on one side listened to the exposition of the Dhamma. Rising

---

[1]A *jhāna* is a state of ecstatic rapture arising from meditation. It is wrongly translated as "trance" by scholars. It is best that the word is left untranslated as the idea is altogether foreign to European religious thought and literature.

[2]From the root *arh* to be worthy, to deserve, etc. It is often left untranslated and in a few instances translated as "Worthy One." Its popular synonym *khīṇāsava* "free from the banes" or "canker-waned" describes the Arahant's chief attribute.

from their seats, they invited him to a meal on the following day and went away. And on the following day, having prepared sumptuous alms and decorated the city, they prepared the road the Buddha was to take, throwing earth where water had eroded it away and thereby making the surface even, and sprinkling sand as white as layers of silver. They strewed puffed grain and flowers, hoisted banners and streamers made of cloth dyed in many colours, and placed arches of banana trees and rows of jars filled to the brim with water. At that time the ascetic Sumedha, rising from his hermitage and proceeding through the air above the spot where those men were at work, saw them joyful and glad; and wishing to investigate its cause he descended from the sky, and standing on one side asked them, "Friends, for whom do you decorate this road?" For it is said:

47. Men of the border districts have invited the Tathāgata; glad at heart they clear the road along which he would come.
48. At that time I left my hermitage and went through the sky with my bark-made garment flapping in the wind.
49. Seeing the multitude overjoyed with fervour, gladdened, and delighted, I then descended from the sky and addressed the men: [**12**]
50. "The great multitude is gladdened, delighted, and overjoyed with fervour; for whom is this path, the common highway being cleared?"

The men replied "Venerable Sumedha, do you not know that Dīpaṅkara, the Lord of ten powers who has attained the perfect Enlightenment and set roll the wheel of the Dhamma is residing in the great monastery Sudassana, having reached our city on his sojourns? We have invited the Blessed One for a meal, and we decorate the route for that the Buddha, our Blessed One will take." The ascetic Sumedha thought, "The very sound of the word "Buddha" is rare in this world, and more so the appearance of a Buddha; it behoves me to join with these folk in clearing the road the Lord of ten powers will take." He then told those men, "If, friends, you are decorating this road for the Buddha, give me also a section so that I will be able to decorate the road along with you." They consented, saying, "Very well," and knowing that the ascetic Sumedha was endowed with psychic powers they decided on a section washed away by water, and assigned it to him saying, "You repair this place." Sumedha who was impelled by the joy arising from thoughts of the Buddha reflected, "I am capable of preparing this spot through my psychic powers; but if it is prepared in that manner it will not give me satisfaction: this day it behoves me to do it by physical exertion"; and he brought earth and threw it on that spot. But even before he could prepare that place, Dīpaṅkara the Lord of ten powers, attended by a retinue of four hundred thousand from among the arahants who had attained the sixfold intuitive knowledge and destroyed their banes, entered that decorated highway with great majesty, in all the immeasurable glory of a Buddha, like a lion on a plateau of red arsenic arousing itself to activity, while deities made offerings such as heavenly garlands and perfumes and celestial choral music resounded, and while men made offerings such as earthly perfumes and garlands. The ascetic Sumedha with wide-open eyes beheld the form of the Lord of ten powers approaching along the decorated highway, endowed with the perfection of beauty, adorned with the thirty-two marks of a Great Being, decked with the eighty minor marks, surrounded by a fathom-deep halo and emitting forth the six coloured mass of Buddha rays resembling flashes of lightning and exuberant diffusion radiating in pairs in a gem coloured sky. He thought, "Today it behoves me to make sacrifice of my life to the Lord of ten powers; let not the Blessed One walk in the swamp. May he, along with his four hundred thousand arahants who have destroyed their banes, go treading on my back as though walking on a bridge of jewelled planks; it will be for my lasting weal and happiness"; and he untied his hair, spread out on the black mud his deer skin, matted locks, [**13**] and bark garment, and lay down in the mire providing as it were a bridge of jewelled planks. For it is said:

51. Questioned by me they replied: "The Conqueror named Dīpaṅkara, the Leader of the world, the incomparable Buddha is born to this world; the path, the common highway is being cleared for him."
52. Hearing the word "Buddha", there arose forthwith in me profound joy; repeating the name "Buddha" over and over I experienced great mental satisfaction.
53. Being delighted and moved with fervour, I reflected standing there: "Here will I sow the seed, let not the moment pass."
54. "If you clear it for the Buddha, assign to me a section; I too will clear the path, the common highway," [I said].
55. They then assigned to me a section of the road to clear. Then repeating in my mind the word "Buddha" I continued to clear the road.
56. Before my section was completed, Dīpaṅkara the great Sage, the Conqueror entered the road, along with four hundred thousand

steadfast sages possessed of sixfold intuitive knowledge, who had destroyed their banes and were pure.

57. Greetings were extended by going forward to meet him, many drums were sounded; men and deities rejoiced and uttered cries of welcome,

58. The deities beheld the mortals and the mortals the deities and both with clasped hands followed the Tathāgata.

59. The deities with their divine music and men with their earthly music, both making their music resound, followed the Tathagata.

60. The deities remaining in mid-air showered down in every direction heavenly *mandārava*[1] flowers, lotuses, and *pāricchatta*[2] flowers.

61. Men standing on the ground scattered upwards in every direction *campaka*,[3] *saḷala*,[4] *nīpa*,[5] ironwood,[6] *punnāga*, and *ketaka*[7] flowers.

62. There did I untie my hair, spread upon the mire the bark garment and the deer skin and lie prostrate [saying:]

63. "May the Buddha, together with his disciples go treading on me. Let him not tread in the mire; it will be for my weal."

Resolution to Gain Enlightenment

Lying upon the mire he again opened his eyes wide, and beholding the majesty of the Buddha Dīpaṅkara, the Lord of ten powers, thought, "If it be my wish I could enter the city of Ramma as a novice in the Order extirpating all the defilements. [**14**] But it does not serve my purpose merely to extirpate the defilements and attain Nibbāna as a man of no consequence. I would rather, like Dīpaṅkara, the Lord of ten powers, attain the highest Enlightenment, and taking mankind aboard

---

[1] *Erythrina fulgens* or coral tree, one of the five celestial trees, also identified as *Erithrina suberosa*.

[2] The coral tree *Erythrina variegata*, another heavenly tree found in Nandana-vana, in Indra's heaven.

[3] The *Champak* or *Michelia champak*, a tree with large fragrant yellowish flowers.

[4] Also spelled *salala*, a fragrant bush.

[5] The *Kadamba* tree or *Nauclea kadamba*.

[6] The *Na* tree or *Mesua ferrea*.

[7] A shrub usually grown for hedges, the screw pine or *pandanus*.

the ship of the Dhamma, ford them across the ocean of Saṃsāra,[1] and afterwards enter into the perfect Nibbāna. This becomes me." Thence with the concurrence of the eight conditions, he made a resolution to become a Buddha and lay down. Therefore it is said:

64. As I lay upon the earth it so occurred to my mind: "If I so wish, today I will burn away my defilements.
65. "What use have I of realising the Dhamma here now, as a man unknown? I will attain Omniscience and become a Buddha for the sake of the multitude with its deities.
66. "What use have I of crossing over all by myself, being fully resolute? I will attain Omniscience and become a Buddha for the sake of the multitude with its deities.
67. "By this resolution of mine, made before the highest of men, I will attain Omniscience and carry across the many folk.
68. "Cutting off the stream of Saṃsāra and destroying the three modes of becoming[2] I will embark in the ship of the Doctrine and ferry across the multitude with its deities."

The Eight Conditions

Since, of him who resolves for Buddhahood,

69. The resolution which consists of a combination of the eight conditions — birth as a human being, the advantage of sex, the good fortune, the meeting with a Teacher, ordination, endowment of latent capabilities to higher knowledge, the dedication of one's life, and resolute will — reaches its fulfilment.

The resolution of a person for Buddhahood made in a human existence is fulfilled. The resolution of a *nāga*,[3] a *supaṇṇa*,[4] or a deity does not reach fulfilment. As a human being too, the resolution of a person in the male sex alone is fulfilled, but not of a woman, a eunuch, or of an hermaphrodite. Even as a man, the resolution of a person who has the capability of attaining arahatship in the same existence is fulfilled, and not of another. In addition to possessing this

---

[1]The cycle of existence or continued round of birth.

[2]The three forms of existence are: *kāma*, *rūpa* and *arūpa*, i.e. sensual, corporeal and formless (see *PED* s.v. *bhava*).

[3]Supernatural or semi-divine beings usually represented as cobras in art.

[4]The natural enemy of the serpents. Mythical winged creatures which feed upon the latter and almost identical with *garuḷa*.

good fortune, the resolution of a person made personally in the presence of the Buddha is fulfilled, but not of a person who resolves near a shrine or at the foot of a Bodhi tree after the passing away of the Buddha. Of him who resolves in the presence of Buddhas it is fulfilled to him only who bears the emblems of a religious mendicant and not to him who remains a layman. Of a religious mendicant too, it is fulfilled to him only who has gained the fivefold insight and the eightfold attainments, but not to him who is devoid of these endowments. Even of him who is endowed with these virtues, it is fulfilled to him alone who possesses service of the nature of making sacrifice of his life for the sake of the Buddhas, but not to another. In addition to the service performed, it is fulfilled to him alone who has great yearning, endeavour, effort, and striving, for the sake of the contributory factors to Enlightenment, but not to another. Here follows a simile to illustrate the magnitude of effort: If there were a person who is capable of crossing by the might of his main the entire sphere of the universe engulfed in one mass of water and going to the farther shore, [15] he is able to attain Englightenment. Or, if there is a person who is capable of going to the farther side, continuing on foot, wading his way through and crushing under foot a bamboo thicket which has overrun the entire world sphere, he is able to attain Enlightenment. Or else, if there be a person who is capable of reaching the farther side, treading with wary step the ground bestrewn all over with points of sharp weapons, the entire surface of the world sphere being dug in with weapons, he is able to attain Enlightenment. Or besides, if there be a person who is capable of reaching the farther side, crumbling under foot the expanse of the entire world sphere overladen with glowing embers, he is able to attain Enlightenment. He who does not consider any of these acts difficult for him to perform, saying, "I will cross this and go, and reach the farther side," and who is endowed with yearning, endeavour, effort, and striving of such magnitude: his resolution is fulfilled, but not of another. Possessing a combination of these eight qualities the ascetic Sumedha made his resolution to attain Enlightenment and lay there.

The Buddha Named Gotama

And the Blessed One Dīpaṅkara came there; and standing near the ascetic Sumedha's head he opened wide his eyes which possessed the fivefold grace, as though opening a jewelled casement, and beholding the ascetic Sumedha who lay upon the mire he investigated through his insight into the future, "This ascetic lies here making his resolution for Buddhahood; will his resolution be fulfilled or not?"; he foresaw that on the elapse of four *asaṅkheyyas* and a hundred thousand æons from then he would become a Buddha named Gotama; and as he stood there he prophesied amidst the assembly: "Do you see this ascetic of austere habits lying on the mud?" "Yes Sir." "He lies here having made a resolution to become a Buddha. His aspiration will come true. He will become a Buddha named Gotama four *asaṅkheyyas* and a hundred thousand æons hence. In that existence his residence will be the city named Kapilavatthu, his mother the queen Māyā, his father the king Suddhodana, his chief disciple the Elder Upatissa, his second leading disciple Kolita, the personal attendant of the Buddha will be Ānanda, his chief female disciple the nun Khemā, and his second leading female disciple the nun Uppalavaṇṇā. With ripened wisdom he will make the Great Renunciation, engage in great exertion and ascending the seat of knowledge at the foot of the Assattha[1] tree attain Enlightenment, having accepted milk-rice at the foot of the Banyan[2] tree and partaken of it on the banks of the river Nerañjarā. For it is said:

70. Dīpankara the knower of the world, the receiver of offerings stood near my head as I lay, and made this pronouncement:
71. "Behold this ascetic of austere habits with his matted locks! Countless æons hence he will become a Buddha in this world. [**16**]
72. The Tathāgata departing from the fair city named after Kapila engaging in great exertion and practising severe austerities,
73. Being seated at the foot of the Ajapāla[3] tree, the Tathāgata will accept the milk-rice there and wend his way to the Nerañjarā river.
74. The Conqueror will partake of his milk-rice on the banks of the Nerañjarā and walk to the foot of the Bodhi tree along the decorated route.
75. The unique Sage of great glory will go round his seat of Enlightenment reverentially, and attain Enlightenment at the foot of the Assattha tree.
76. His mother who gives him birth will bear the name Māyā, his father that of Suddhodana, and he will be called Gotama.
77. Kolita and Upatissa who are free from the banes and from all attachments, with restrained minds and collected at heart, will become his two chief disciples.
78. Ānanda will be the servitor who will attend on the Conqueror, Khemā and Uppalavaṇṇā will become his chief female disciples.
79. They will be free from the banes and from all attachment, their

---

[1] *Ficus religiosa* or Bo tree.

[2] *Ficus bengalensis*, Sinhalese *nuga*.

[3] The Goatherd banyan tree on the banks of the river Nerañjara (see s.v. in *DPPN*).

minds will be restrained and they will be collected at heart. The tree of Enlightenment of the Blessed One will be known as Assattha."

The Portents

The ascetic Sumedha was greatly overjoyed to learn that his aspirations would be fulfilled. The multitude too was overcome with joy when they heard the word of Dīpaṅkara, the Lord of ten powers, that the ascetic Sumedha was an embryonic Buddha, a Buddha-sapling. They further thought: "Just as a man who is about to cross a river, when he finds it difficult to cross over to the ford directly opposite him, lands at a ford lower down, so as we are unable to attain the paths and their fruits in the dispensation of Dīpaṅkara, the Lord of ten powers, let us have the ability to realize the paths and their fruits under you when you become a Buddha in the future!" So saying they made their aspirations. The Lord of the ten powers, Dīpaṅkara, himself lauded the Bodhisatta and honoured him with eight handfuls of flowers and went his way having walked round him reverentially. Those four hundred thousand canker-waned sages too honoured the Bodhisatta with offerings of perfumes and garlands and departed going round him reverentially. The deities and the men themselves honoured him likewise, worshipped and departed. When all had departed the Bodhisatta rose from where he lay and sat down cross-legged on the heap of flowers thinking of examining the Perfections. When the Bodhisatta was thus seated the deities of the entire ten thousand world spheres assembled shouting applause and praised the Bodhisatta in all manner of exaltation, saying "O venerable ascetic Sumedha, all those portents which manifested themselves when Bodhisattas of yore were seated cross-legged with the intention of examining the Perfections: all of them have appeared today. There is no doubt that you will become a Buddha. [17] We know it for certain. He for whose benefit these omens appear will undoubtedly become a Buddha. May you make firm your effort and strive hard." For it is said:

80. Hearing these words of the incomparable and mighty Sage, the men and deities were delighted and exclaimed: "Here is a Buddha seedling!"
81. The inhabitants of the ten thousand worlds together with the deities cheered aloud clapping their hands, laughed with joy and adored him with clasped hands.

82. [They said:] "Should we not succeed in the dispensation of this Lord of the world, we would, in a future age go before him.
83. "Just as men who swim a river, reach a lower ford and cross over the great waters when they fail to reach the ford opposite them,
84. "So, all of us will go before him in a future age, if this Conqueror's dispensation we miss."
85. Dīpaṅkara, the knower of the world, the receiver of offerings, praised my action and raised his right foot to depart.
86. All those sons of the Conqueror who were there walked around me reverentially. Men, *nāgas*, and *gandhabbas*[1] saluted me and departed.
87. When the Leader of the world together with his followers had disappeared from sight, overjoyed and with joyful heart I then rose from my seat.
88. Happiness pervaded me, delight suffused me, joy enlivened me; and then I sat cross-legged.
89. Thereupon, seated cross-legged I reflected: "I have mastered the *jhānas* and reached perfection in intuitive knowledge.
90. "In the thousandfold[2] world there are no sages, my equals; in psychic phenomena I am unequalled and such bliss have I attained."
91. When I seated myself cross-legged the dwellers of the ten thousand worlds raised a tumultuous hue, saying "You certainly will become a Buddha!
92. "The omens that were seen when Bodhisattas of yore seated themselves cross-legged: they are seen today.
93. "Cold is dispelled, heat is allayed; these omens are seen today: you certainly will become a Buddha.
94. "The ten thousand world systems are silent and motionless; these omens are seen today: you certainly will become a Buddha, [**18**]
95. "High winds do not blow, streams do not flow; these omens are seen today: you certainly will become a Buddha.
96. "Forthwith bloom flowers sprung on land and in water; today all of them have bloomed: you certainly will become a Buddha.

---

[1]Heavenly musicians.

[2]Read *sāhassikamhi lokamhi*, "in the universe consisting of a thousand worlds", as in *dasasahassī lokadhātu*.

97. "All creepers and trees are at the same time laden with fruit; today all of them are fruit-bearing: you certainly will become a Buddha.
98. "Jewels suspended above or placed on the ground sparkle together; today those jewels sparkle: you certainly will become a Buddha,
99. "Simultaneously are heard strains of earthly and heavenly music; both of them sound forth today: you certainly will become a Buddha.
100. "Forthwith shower down from the sky flowers of delightful hue; today they fall incessantly: you certainly will become a Buddha.
101. "The mighty ocean bends low, and ten thousand worlds quake; today they resound with a din: you certainly will become a Buddha.
102. "Ten thousand fires in hell are extinguished instantaneously; today those fires are quenched: you certainly will become a Buddha.
103. "The sun shines bright and all the stars are visible; today they are to be seen: you certainly will become a Buddha.
104. "Instantaneously water gushes forth from the earth where no rain has fallen; it continues to gush forth from the earth: you certainly will become a Buddha.
105. "Myriads of stars and the asterisms shine in the vault of heaven; the asterism of Visākha is in conjunction with the moon: you certainly will become a Buddha.
106. "Creatures that live in hollows and caves have gone forth from their lairs; this day they have left their lairs: you certainly will become a Buddha.
107. "There is no discontent among beings, they are now contented; this day all of them are contented: you certainly will become a Buddha.
108. "Diseases now are allayed, and hunger has vanished; this day they are no more to be seen: you certainly will become a Buddha.
109. "Passion now is at its ebb, hatred and delusion have disappeared; this day they have all vanished: you certainly will become a Buddha.
110. "Fear does not exist any more, for this is what obtains today. By that sign we know that you certainly will become a Buddha.
111. "No dust is stirred upward, for this is to be seen today. By that sign we know that you certainly will become a Buddha.
112. "Foul smell recedes, a heavenly fragrance pervades; such fragrance emanates today: you certainly will become a Buddha. [**19**]
113. "All the deities other than the formless are manifest; all of them are seen this day: you certainly will become a Buddha.

114. "As many as are the hells, all of them are seen forthwith; all of them are seen this day: you certainly will become a Buddha.
115. "Walls and doorways and rocks form no barriers now; all of them have turned into space; you certainly will become a Buddha.
116. "No death nor birth takes place at this time; such a state is seen this day: you certainly will become a Buddha.
117. "Make firm your effort, do not go back, go forward. We know this for certain that you will become a Buddha."

The Bodhisatta was greatly encouraged when he heard the words of Dīpaṅkara, the Lord of ten powers, and of the deities of the ten thousand world spheres; and he reflected, "Buddhas indeed, make no empty statements; there is no deviation in the statements of Buddhas. Even as it is certain and must necessarily happen that the clod of earth thrown into the air should fall, as death comes to the born, as sunrise follows the setting in of the dawn, as a lion roars its lion's roar when it leaves the lair, as a woman delivers her child when she is in an advanced state of pregnancy, even so the statements of Buddhas are sure to come true and cannot fail. Assuredly, I will become a Buddha." For it is said:

118. Having heard the words of the Buddha as well as of the deities of the ten thousand world spheres, gladdened and overjoyed, I then thought thus:
119. "There is no duplicity in the words of the Buddhas, the Conquerors do not utter empty words, there is no falsehood in the Buddhas: I certainly will become a Buddha.
120. "Even as a clod hurled into the sky, for certainty falls to the ground, even so, the words of the great Buddhas are eternal and sure.
121. "Even as death to all creatures is assured and is for all time, even so the words of the great Buddhas are eternal and sure.
122. "Even as the sunrise is certain when night fades into day, even so the words of the great Buddhas are eternal and sure.
123. "Even as the roaring of the lion that has left its lair is certain, even so the words of the great Buddhas are eternal and sure.
124. "Even as the delivery is certain to those who are about to bring forth young, even so the words of the great Buddha are eternal and sure."

The Contributory Conditions to Enlightenment: The Perfection of Generosity

Having thus made his resolution, "I will certainly become a Buddha," he searched in due course the entire cosmic order in order to investigate the contributory conditions to Enlightenment, saying, "Where are the contributory conditions to Enlightenment? [**20**] Are they above or below, or in the principal or the intermediate directions?"; and he beheld the first Perfection, of Generosity, which was practised and followed by former Bodhisattas. And he admonished himself thus: "O Wise Sumedha, from now on fulfil the first Perfection of Generosity. Just as an overturned water-pot discharges its water holding back nothing and drawing in nothing, so by giving everything in charity to supplicants that come to you, each according to his wish, holding back nothing, without regard to wealth or fame or wife and child or one limb or the other of the body, you will become a Buddha, seated at the foot of the Bodhi tree." Saying so he firmly resolved on the first Perfection of Generosity. For it is said:

125. Well now, I search here and there, above, below, or in the ten directions, as far as the cosmic order prevails, for the contributory conditions to Enlightenment.
126. Then in my search I saw the first Perfection of Generosity, the great highway followed by the mighty sages of the past.
127. Firstly, make firm and take upon yourself the Perfection of Generosity and proceed, if you wish to attain Enlightenment.
128. Just as a pot full to the brim when overturned by someone discharges all its water and holds nothing back in it,
129. So, seeing supplicants whether high or low or middling, give away everything in charity, like the overturned pot.

The Perfection of Morality

As he investigated further, saying, "This alone cannot possibly constitute the contributory conditions to Enlightenment," he saw the second Perfection, of Morality, and thought, "O Wise Sumedha, from now on fulfil the Perfection of Morality as well. Just as a *camarī* antelope protects its tail regardless of its life, so you too from now on, regardless even of life, guard your Morality, and become a Buddha."

Reflecting thus he firmly resolved on the second Perfection, of Morality. For it is said:

130. Not indeed will these alone be the conditions for Enlightenment. I will look for those other conditions as well which ripen in Enlightenment.
131. Then in my search I saw the second Perfection, of Morality, the great highway followed by the mighty sages of the past.
132. "Secondly, make firm and take upon yourself this Perfection of Morality and proceed, if you wish to attain Enlightenment.
133. "Just as a *camarī* antelope reaches death when its tail is entangled in some object, but does not injure the tail, [**21**]
134. "So, having perfected the moral precepts in their four spheres, always guard your morality as the *camarī* its tail."

The Perfection of Renunciation

As he investigated further, saying, "These alone cannot possibly constitute the contributory conditions to Enlightenment," he saw the third Perfection, of Renunciation, and thought, "O Wise Sumedha, from now on fulfil the Perfection of Renunciation as well. Just as a man serving a long sentence in prison feels no love for it, but is disgusted with it and does not wish to live there any longer, so you too should be desirous of escaping from all states of becoming, considering them as prisons; and being disgusted with them you proceed in the direction of renunciation and thus become a Buddha." Reflecting thus he firmly resolved on the third Perfection, of Renunciation. For it is said:

135. Not indeed will these alone be the conditions for Enlightenment. I will look for those other conditions as well which ripen in Enlightenment.
136. Then in my search I saw the third Perfection, of Renunciation, the great highway followed by the mighty sages of the past.
137. "Thirdly, make firm and take upon yourself this Perfection of Renunciation, and proceed, if you wish to attain Enlightenment.
138. "Just as a man who has lived long in the prison-house, tormented with suffering, forms no attachment to it but is eager for his release,

139. "So look upon all states of becoming as prisons and proceed in the direction of renunciation to obtain release from becoming."

The Perfection of Wisdom

As he investigated further, saying, "These alone cannot possibly constitute the contributory conditions to Enlightenment," he saw the fourth Perfection, of Wisdom, and thought, "O Wise Sumedha, from now on fulfil the Perfection of Wisdom as well. Without avoiding any one among the small, middling, and exalted, do you approach all wise men and ask them questions. Just as a mendicant friar on his begging round goes to each one in due order avoiding none of the families in the various categories beginning with the poor, and obtains in no time the food for his sustenance, so approach all wise men, and asking them questions become a Buddha." Reflecting thus he firmly resolved on the fourth Perfection, of Wisdom. For it is said:

140. Not indeed will these alone be the conditions for Enlightenment. I will look for those other conditions as well which ripen in Enlightenment.
141. Then in my search I saw the fourth Perfection, of Wisdom, the great highway followed by the mighty sages of the past.
142. "Fourthly, make firm and take upon yourself the Perfection of Wisdom and proceed, if you wish to attain Enlightenment. [**22**]
143. "Just as a mendicant friar, while begging his food obtains his sustenance without avoiding the houses of the rich, poor or the middling,
144. "So, reach the Perfection of Wisdom by constantly questioning the wise men and attain Enlightenment."

The Perfection of Effort

As he investigated further, saying, "This alone cannot possibly constitute the contributory conditions to Enlightenment," he saw the fifth Perfection, of Effort, and thought, "O Wise Sumedha, from now on fulfil the Perfection of Effort as well. Just as the lion, the king of beasts, exhibits great energy in all its postures, so exhibit strenuous exertion with unabated energy in all your postures in every state of becoming, and become a Buddha." Reflecting thus he firmly resolved on the fifth Perfection, of Effort. For it is said:

145. Not indeed will these alone be the conditions for Enlightenment. I will look for those other conditions as well which ripen in Enlightenment.
146. Then in my search I saw the fifth Perfection, of Effort, the great highway followed by the mighty sages of the past.
147. "Fifthly, make firm and take upon yourself this Perfection of Effort and proceed, if you wish to attain Enlightenment.
148. "Just as the lion the king of beasts, in its postures of sitting, standing, and walking, exhibits unabated vigour and is always courageous at heart,
149. "So make firm your effort in all states of becoming, reach the Perfection of Effort and attain Enlightenment."

The Perfection of Patience

As he investigated further, saying, "These alone cannot possibly constitute the contributory conditions to Enlightenment," he saw the sixth Perfection, of Patience, and thought, "O Wise Sumedha, from now on fulfil the Perfection of Patience as well; be indifferent in both praise and censure. Just as things both pure and impure are cast upon the earth, and the earth on that account shows neither pleasure nor displeasure, but bears them up, suffers them, and endures them, so be indifferent equally to both praise and censure, and become a Buddha." Reflecting thus he firmly resolved on the sixth Perfection, of Patience. For it is said:

150. Not indeed will these alone be the conditions for Enlightenment. I will look for those other conditions as well which ripen in Enlightenment.
151. "Then in my search I saw the sixth Perfection, of Patience, the great highway followed by the mighty sages of the past.
152. "Sixthly, make firm and take this upon yourself. With undivided attention in it you will attain perfect Enlightenment. [**23**]
153. "Just as the earth suffers all that is thrown upon it, both pure and impure and shows no resentment nor love,
154. "So while enduring the praise or reproach of every one reach the Perfection of Patience and attain Enlightenment.

The Perfection of Truth

As he investigated further, saying, "These alone cannot possibly constitute the contributory conditions to Enlightenment," he saw the seventh Perfection, of Truth, and thought, "O Wise Sumedha, from now on fulfil the Perfection of Truth as well. Even though the thunderbolt may descend upon your head, do not utter a conscious lie for the sake of wealth and so forth, being actuated by desire and like motives. Just as the "healing star" Venus pursues its own course through all the seasons without running along a different orbit, so you too, without forsaking the truth and uttering no falsehood, will become a Buddha." Reflecting thus he firmly resolved on the seventh Perfection, of Truth. For it is said:

155. Not indeed will these alone be the conditions for Enlightenment. I will look for those other conditions as well which ripen in Enlightenment.
156. Then in my search I saw the seventh Perfection, of Truth, the great highway followed by the mighty sages of the past.
157. "Seventhly, make firm and take this upon yourself. With no duplicity in speech regarding it, you will attain perfect Enlightenment.
158. "Just as the 'healing-star' held evenly balanced by the world with its deities, does not deviate from its course in varying season, time or year,[1]
159. "So depart not from your course in things truthful. Having reached the Perfection of Truth you will attain Enlightenment."

The Perfection of Resolution

As he investigated further, saying "These alone cannot possibly constitute the contributory conditions to Enlightenment," he saw the eighth Perfection, of Resolution, and thought, "O Wise Sumedha, from now on fulfil the Perfection of Resolution as well. Be steadfast in whatever resolution you make. As a rock, even while the wind beats upon it on every side, does not tremble nor quake but remains in its own place, likewise be unshaken in your resolution and become a Buddha." Reflecting thus he firmly resolved on the eighth Perfection, of Resolution. For it is said:

---

[1]Read *utuvasse vā* as in SHB.

160. Not indeed will these alone be the conditions for Enlightenment. I will look for those other conditions as well which ripen in Enlightenment. [**24**]
161. Then in my search I saw the eighth Perfection, of Resolution, the great highway followed by the mighty sages of the past.
162. "Eighthly, make firm and take this upon yourself. Being unshaken therein you will attain perfect Enlightenment.
163. "Just as a rocky mountain stable and standing firm is not moved with strong winds, but remains in its place,
164. "So be always steadfast in your resolution. Having reached the Perfection of Resolution you will attain Enlightenment."

The Perfection of Amity

As he investigated further, saying, "These alone cannot possibly constitute the contributory conditions to Enlightenment," he saw the ninth Perfection, of Amity, and thought, "O Wise Sumedha, from now on fulfil the Perfection of Amity as well. Be of the same frame of mind towards those who are well and ill disposed towards you. As water extends its coolness equally alike to both the wicked and the virtuous, you too remain with the same frame of mind, with thoughts of love towards all creatures, and become a Buddha." Reflecting thus he firmly resolved on the ninth Perfection, of Amity. For it is said:

165. Not indeed will these alone be the conditions for Enlightenment. I will look for those other conditions as well which ripen in Enlightenment.
166. Then in my search I saw the ninth Perfection, of Amity, the great highway followed by the mighty sages of the past.
167. "Ninthly, make firm and take this upon yourself. Be unrivalled in friendliness, if you wish to attain Enlightenment.
168. "Just as water suffuses with its coolness both the virtuous and the wicked alike, and washes away dust and impurity,
169. "So develop thoughts of friendliness to friend and foe alike. Having reached the Perfection of Amity you will attain Enlightenment.

The Perfection of Equanimity

As he investigated further, saying, "These alone cannot possibly constitute the contributory conditions to Enlightenment," he saw the tenth Perfection, of Equanimity, and thought, "O Wise Sumedha, from now on fulfil the Perfection of Equanimity as well. Be unperturbed in both prosperity and adversity. As the earth remains indifferent when both pure and impure matter is thrown upon it, you too remain unperturbed in both prosperity and adversity and become a Buddha." Reflecting thus he firmly resolved on the tenth Perfection, of Equanimity. For it is said: [**25**]

170. Not indeed will these alone be the conditions for Enlightenment. I will look for those other conditions as well which ripen in Enlightenment.
171. Then in my search I saw the tenth Perfection, of Equanimity, the great highway followed by the mighty sages of the past.
172. "Tenthly, make firm and take this upon yourself. Being evenly balanced and firm, you will attain Enlightenment.
173. "Just as the earth is devoid of hatred or liking and bears with equanimity what is cast upon it, both pure and impure,
174. "So always be evenly balanced in both happiness and sorrow. Having gained the Perfection of Equanimity you will attain Enlightenment."

The Perfections

He next reflected, "These alone in this world are the contributory conditions to Enlightenment which mature in Enlightenment and have to be fulfilled by Bodhisattas. And besides these ten Perfections there are no others. These ten Perfections are neither in the sky above, nor on the earth below, nor in the quarters commencing with the East, but they are rooted within my heart." Having thus realized the fact of their being established in the heart, he firmly resolved on them; and grasping them firmly again and again he mastered them in their progressive and regressive orders. Taking them at the end he brought them back to the beginning, taking them at the beginning he took them forward to the end; taking them at the centre he concluded at the two ends and taking them at the two extremities he concluded at the centre.

The Earth Trembles

Thinking that the sacrifice of limb is like unto the Perfections, that of worldly possessions to the Sub-perfections, and that of life to the Supreme Perfections, he mastered the ten Perfections, the ten Sub-perfections, and the ten Supreme Perfections, like one making an emulsion of two kindred oils or churning up the great ocean skirting the universe using the mighty peak Meru as the churning rod. As he continued to master the ten Perfections, by the power of his virtue this great earth four *nahutas*[1] and two hundred thousand *yojanas*[2] in thickness trembled, shook, and quaked making a mighty roar, like a sheaf of reeds trodden by an elephant or a sugar mill with pressure applied to it; and it spun round and round like a potter's wheel or the wheel of an oil-mill. Therefore it is said:

175. "These alone in the world are the conditions which ripen in Enlightenment. Beyond these there are no others; establish yourself firmly in them."
176. As he mastered these conditions characterised by their natural and intrinsic qualities, the earth trembled ten thousand fold by the power of his virtue.
177. The earth trembled and resounded like a sugar mill with pressure applied, or like the wheel of an oil-mill; thus did the earth quake. [**26**]

The Buddha Named Gotama

While the earth was trembling the dwellers of the city of Ramma who were unable to endure it fainted and fell like large Sāla[3] trees struck down by the high winds that prevail at the destruction of the world; water-pots and other vessels fashioned by potters kept on revolving and were reduced to fragments by striking against each other. The people, agitated with fear, went up to the Teacher and asked him, "What, O Lord, is this turmoil caused by *nāgas* or by any others among the spirits, demons, deities, and others? We do not know what it is all

---

[1]A *nahuta* is a very large number: a "myriad".

[2]A *yoyana* is a length of distance, a "league". This is reckoned as the distance a team of horses can draw a chariot without tiring (see s.v. in *PED*).

[3]*Shorea robusta*, the national tree of the Sakyas.

about." The Teacher listened to what they said and replied, "Fear not, be not disturbed. There is no danger arising to you from this. The Wise Sumedha, to whom this day I have predicted that he will in the future become the Buddha named Gotama, is now reflecting on the Perfections. As he reflects on the Perfections and examines them thoroughly the entire ten thousand world system trembles simultaneously, and resounds by the power of his virtue." For it is said:

178. All those who had gathered at the Buddha's refectory, trembled and lay prone on the ground there, falling in a swoon.
179. Many thousands of water pots and many hundreds of other vessels were reduced to powder and were scattered about there by being dashed against each other.
180. The multitudes, excited, trembling, frightened, agitated, and confused in mind, assembled together and visited the Buddha Dīpaṅkara.
181. [They asked him:] "What will befall the world, some good or evil? The whole world is afflicted. O discerning Sage, ward off that harm."
182. The great Sage Dīpaṅkara then pacified them: "Be calm, fear not at this trembling of the earth.
183. "He of whom I have prophesied this day that he will become a Buddha in the world, now reflects on the phenomena which Conquerors of yore have followed.
184. "As he reflects on these phenomena, the complete ken of Enlightenment, the earth of the ten thousand world systems with their deities has trembled."

Songs of Praise

The multitude too, overflowing with joy on hearing the words of the Tathāgata, left the city of Ramma taking with them garlands, perfumes, and ointments and went to the Bodhisatta. They made gifts of those garlands and other articles and worshipped him, and having walked reverentially round him, they returned to the city of Ramma. The Bodhisatta himself made his firm resolution for the fulfillment of the ten Perfections and rose from his seat. For it is said: **[27]**

185. No sooner they heard the words of the Buddha than were their minds reassured. All of them came to me and paid homage once again.

186. Thereupon, having taken upon myself the qualities leading to Enlightenment, with firm mental resolve I saluted Dīpaṅkara and then rose from my seat.

Then the deities of all the thousand world spheres assembled and honoured the Bodhisatta with garlands and perfumes as he rose from his seat, and uttered words of praise and blessing such as, "O venerable ascetic Sumedha, this day you have made a great resolution at the feet of Dīpaṅkara, the Lord of ten powers; may you accomplish it without any hindrance, let no fear nor trepidation arise in you, let not the slightest ailment come upon your body, may you in no time fulfil the Perfections and realize perfect Enlightenment. Just as flowering and fruit-bearing trees flower and bear their fruits in season, so you too, without exceeding your time limit, will soon embrace the supreme Enlightenment." Having thus uttered these words they returned each one to his divine abode. The Bodhisatta too, being thus praised by the deities, made firm his resolve strenuously thinking that after having accomplished the ten Perfections he would become a Buddha four *asaṅkheyyas* and a hundred thousand æons from then; and rising into the sky returned to the Himalayas. For it is said:

187. As he rose from his seat both deities and men scattered celestial and earthly flowers.
188. Both deities and men conferred their blessing with the words: "Great is your resolution, attain it as desired.
189. May all calamities subside and grief and illness perish; let no harm befall you. May you ere long attain the highest Enlightenment.
190. Just as flowering trees blossom when the season arrives, so may you, O great hero, blossom forth with the knolwedge of Enlightenment.
191. As did all the highest Enlightened Ones fulfil the ten Perfections, may you as well, O great hero, fulfil the ten Perfections.
192. As do all the highest Enlightened Ones gain awakening at the seat of Enlightenment, so may you, O great hero, gain awakening at the seat of Enlightenment.
193. As did all the highest Enlightened Ones set rolling the wheel of the Dhamma, so may you, O great hero, set rolling the wheel of the Dhamma.

194. Just as the moon on the full moon might shine in all its purity, so may you, with your ambitions achieved, be resplendent in the ten thousand worlds. [**28**]
195. As the sun released from Rāhu[1] dazzles forth with its heat, so may you be released from the world and shine forth in glory.
196. Just as all the rivers flow into the great ocean, so may the inhabitants of the world, together with the deities, congregate before you."
197. Being thus praised and extolled by them, he took upon himself the ten virtues, and fulfilling them entered the great forest.

Here ends the story of Sumedha.

THE ASSURANCES

Dīpaṅkara

And so the dwellers of the city of Ramma returned to their city and held a large alms-giving to the Brotherhood of monks with the Buddha at its head. The Teacher preached to them the Doctrine and established the multitude in the refuges and so forth; and departing from the city of Ramma, he discharged afterwards all the obligations of a Buddha till the end of his life and in due course passed away in the element of Nibbāna which is free from any material substratum. All that has to be said with reference to it should be understood as stated in the Buddhavaṃsa.[2] For it is stated there:

198. There they entertained the Leader of the world together with the Brotherhood and sought the refuge of the Teacher Dīpaṅkara.
199. The Tathāgata established some in the refuges, some in the five precepts, and others in the ten precepts.
200. To some he gave ordination with its fourfold fruits in the highest plane,[3] to some the unique methods of analytical knowledge.[4]

---

[1]This refers to a solar eclipse. In Indian mythology the demon Rāhu is said to swallow the heavenly bodies during an eclipse.

[2]Bv II, 189*ff.*

[3]These are the "fruits" of four stages in the attainment of *nibbāna*, at which the practitioner becomes a "stream-winner" (*sotāpanna*), a "once-returner" (*sakad-āgāmī*), a "non-returner" (*anāgāmī*) and an arahant.

[4]*paṭisambhidā*: see *PED* s.v.

201. The hero among men conferred on some the eight noble attainments[1] and on some others the three wisdoms and the sixfold intuitive knowledge.[2]
202. In this manner the Great Sage instructed the multitude. Thereby the dispensation of the Lord of the world became widespread.
203. He of the mighty jaw and taurine chest, Dīpaṅkara by name, saved the many folk and released them from their evil bourn.
204. Having seen even a hundred *yojanas* away folk who can be awakened, the Great Sage would go there in an instant and enlighten them.
205. At the first conversion the Lord Buddha awakened a hundred crores, and at the second a hundred thousand [crores].
206. When the Buddha preached the Doctrine in the abode of the devas, there took place the third conversion of ninety thousand crores. [**29**]
207. The Teacher Dīpaṅkara had three congregations, the first assembly consisted of a hundred thousand crores.
208. Again, when the conqueror went into seclusion on Nārada peak there assembled a hundred crores of arahants, stainless and bane-free.
209. When the Great Hero dwelt on the Sudassana promontory the Sage then was surrounded by ninety thousand crores.
210. At that time I was a matted-hair ascetic of severe penance, able to wander through the sky, having reached mastery in the fivefold intuitive knowledge.[3]

---

[1]These are the eight stages of meditation: see *PED* s.v. *samāpatti.*

[2]The "three wisdoms" are: (i) the divine eye (*dibbacakkhu*), which sees the death and rebirth of beings, (ii) the memory of former lives (*pubbenivāsānussati-ñāṇa*) and (iii) knowledge of the extinction of corruptions (or "cankers", "banes") (*āsava-khaya-ñāṇa*), to these are added magical powers (*iddhi*), the divine ear (*dibba-sota*), and knowledge of others' minds (*ceto-pariya-ñāṇa*) to give the "sixfold intuitive knowledge". Sometimes only five *abhiññā* are mentioned, as in stanza 210, when the "supermundane" (*lokuttara*) attainment of knowledge of the extinction of corruptions, (equivalent to the attainment of Arahantship) is omitted and only the five "mundane" (*lokiya*) attainments given.

[3]See previous note, Sumedha could not attain Arahantship since he could not then have gone on to become Buddha Gotama.

211. There was the realization of the Dhamma to tens and twenties of thousands; those that occurred in ones and twos were beyond all reckoning.
212. The dispensation of the Blessed One Dīpaṅkara was widespread, shared by many, prosperous, flourishing, and perfectly purified.
213. Four hundred thousand endowed with the sixfold intuitive knowledge and of great psychic power always surrounded Dīpaṅkara, the knower of the world.
214. Among those in the path of training at that time, whoever left human existence without achieving their ambition were themselves certainly to be blamed.
215. The teaching was made efflorescent by the steadfast arahants who were stainless and free from the banes, and it shone in the world with its deities.
216. The city of the Teacher Dīpaṅkara was Rammavatī by name, his father the Khattiya[1] Sumedha, and his mother Sumedhā.
217. The two chief disciples of the Teacher Dīpaṅkara were Sumaṅgala and Tissa and his personal attendant was Sāgata.
218. Nandā and Sunandā were his chief women disciples and the Pipphalī tree[2] was called the Bodhi tree of that Blessed One.
219. The Great Sage Dīpaṅkara was eighty cubits in height, and he shone like a Dīpa tree[3] or a lordly Sāla in blossom.
220. The life-span of the Great Sage was hundred thousand years. As long as he remained on earth he forded great multitudes across.
221. Having illuminated the good Teaching, and having forded the multitude across, he flamed like a mass of fire and with his disciples passed away in Nibbāna.
222. That psychic power, that glory and those precious wheels on the feet[4] — all of them have disappeared. Are not all constituent elements void? [**30**]

---

[1]I.e. "nobleman", "king", "warrior".

[2]The pipal tree, same as *Assattha* (Bo), *ficus religosa*.

[3]The Sinhalese paraphrase (*sanne*) says this was a lamp-stand. (*Dīpa* can mean a "light"). *Dīparukkha* here probably means a deodar pine.

[4]These are one of the "thirty-two marks of a Great Man" (i.e. a Buddha), *mahāpurisa-lakkhaṇāni.*

Koṇḍañña

223. Subsequent to Dīpaṅkara was the Leader named Koṇḍañña of immense majesty and unlimited glory, immeasurable and unassailable.[1]

Vijitāvī

Subsequent to the Blessed One Dīpaṅkara the Teacher named Koṇḍañña appeared after the elapse of an innumerable world-period, He too had three assemblies of disciples: at the first assembly there were a hundred thousand crores, at the second a thousand crores, and at the third ninety crores. At that time the Bodhisatta was born as the universal monarch Vijitāvī; he held a magnificent alms giving to the Brotherhood of monks, a hundred thousand crores in number, at whose head was the Buddha. The Teacher prophesied that the Bodhisatta would become a Buddha and preached the Doctrine. Having listened to the discourse of the Teacher he abdicated his throne and sought ordination. He studied the three Piṭakas and evolved the eight attainments and the fivefold intuitive knowledge, and without failing in the *jhānas* he was reborn in the world of Brahmā. The city of the Buddha Koṇḍañña was called Rammavatī, the Khattiya Sunanda was his father, the queen Sujātā his mother, Bhadda and Subhadda his two chief disciples, and Anuruddha his personal attendant, Tissā and Upatissā his chief women disciples, and the tree Sālakalyāṇi[2] his Bodhi. His body was eighty cubits high and his life-span a hundred thousand years.

Maṅgala

After him, at the elapse of an innumerable world period, four Buddhas — Maṅgala, Sumana, Revata, and Sobhita — appeared in one and the same æon. The Blessed One Maṅgala had three assemblies of disciples. Among them, at the first assembly there were a hundred thousand crores of monks, at the second a thousand crores, and at the third ninety crores. His step-brother Ānanda, with a retinue of ninety crores, went to the Teacher's presence to listen to the doctrine. The Teacher delivered a discourse dealing gradually with the various topics

---

[1]Bv III, I.

[2]The same as *sāla*.

commencing from the beginning. Together with his retinue he attained arahantship and gained the fourfold analytical knowledge. As the Teacher directed his vision on the former deeds of those clansmen, he perceived their good fortune to receive bowls and robes by supernatural means, and said, "Come ye Brethren," stretching out his right hand. Instantaneously, all of them bearing bowls and robes miraculously obtained and endowed with deportment like Elders of sixty years' religious experience worshipped the Teacher and stood around him. This was his third assembly of disciples.

Whereas with other Buddhas their bodily radiance spreads around to the distance of eighty cubits, it was not so with him, for the radiance of that Blessed One remained all the time suffusing the ten thousand world systems. Trees, the earth, mountains, oceans, and the like, not excepting cooking pots and so forth, appeared as though covered with a film of gold. And his life span was ninety thousand years. All this while, the moon, the sun, and other heavenly bodies were not able to shine by their own radiance. The distinction between night and day was not felt. [**31**] The beings went about their business at all times in the light of the Buddha as they do by day in the light of the sun. The people realized the distinction between night and day from the flowers that bloom in the evening and the birds and such creatures that sing at early dawn. Do not the other Buddhas also possess this power? It is not that they do not: if they so wish they could fill with their radiance the ten thousand world systems or more. But on the other hand, as a result of a former resolution of the Blessed One Maṅgala, his bodily radiance remained permanently filling the ten thousand world systems even as that of other Buddhas was confined to the depth of a fathom.

The *Yakkha* Kharadāṭhika

During his career as a Bodhisatta, in his existence corresponding to that of Vessantara, he, together with his wife and children dwelt on a mountain similar to the Vaṅka Rock. Thereupon a *yakkha*[1] by the name of Kharadāṭhika (Rough Fangs) hearing of the Great Being's inclination towards charity went to him in the guise of a brahmin and asked him for

[1]*Yakkha* — a supernatural being, a follower of Vessavaṇa. In this instance he is a demon, but *yakkha* and demon are not identical.

his two children. The Great Being, who was overjoyed with the thought of giving his children to the brahmin, gave both his children away and made the great earth up to its ocean limits tremble. The *yakkha* stood by the reclining board at the end of the cloister and devoured the two children like a bundle of lotus roots while the Great Being looked on. No grief, not even to the extent of a hair's tip, arose in the Great Being as he looked at the *yakkha* and saw his mouth when he opened it disgorging a stream of blood like a flame. But great joy and satisfaction rose from within his body as he reflected on the well-conferred gift. And he made a resolution that by the resultant force of that deed in his future life rays might go forth from his body in the manner described. As a result of that resolution of his, rays went forth from his body and suffused such a vast region.

There yet was another deed done in a previous existence. It is said that when he was a Bodhisatta he saw a shrine erected for a Buddha, and thinking that he should sacrifice his life to that Buddha he wrapped his whole body in the manner of making a torch. Filling with clarified butter a golden bowl marked with designs of flower buds worked in jewels on it and worth a hundred thousand, he lit a thousand wicks in it; and having set fire to his whole body he spent all night pacing reverentially round the shrine carrying the bowl on his head. In spite of his night-long struggle which lasted till dawn, not even a hair-root was heated, but it appeared as though he was encased in the calyx of a lotus. This indeed is the Dhamma which guards him who guards it.[1] For the Blessed One has said:

224. The Dhamma, forsooth, guards him who conducts himself virtuously, for the Dhamma well followed brings bliss in its train. This is the advantage of the Dhamma well practised, and the virtuous man goes to no evil state.[2] [**32**]

Suruci

On account of the resultant force of this action too, the bodily radiance of that Blessed One remained pervading the ten thousand world systems. At that time our Bodhisatta was born as the brahman

---

[1]The word *dhamma* here refers to *dhammatā*, "the nature of things".

[2]See S I 42.

Suruci; he listened to an exquisite discourse when he went to invite the Teacher for a meal, and said to him "Sir, may it please you to accept a meal from me tomorrow."

"Brahman, how many monks do you wish for?"

"Sir, how many monks are there in your retinue?"

At that time there was only the first assembly of disciples; and accordingly he replied, "A hundred thousand crores."

"Sir, partake of meals at my house along with all of them."

The Teacher consented. The brahman having invited them, thought on his way home, "It is not that I will not be able to give gruel, food, clothes, and other articles to so many monks, but how will there be room for them to sit down?"

Then this reflection of his caused the throne of white marble of Sakka the king of the deities, situated eighty-four thousand *yojanas* above, to become heated. Then Sakka directed his divine vision, thinking, "Who is it that wants me to leave this place?" He beheld the Great Being and thought, "The brahman Suruci has invited the Brotherhood of monks with the Buddha at its head and is concerned over a place to seat them. It is fit that I should go there and obtain a share of the merit." He then assumed the guise of a builder, and carrying adze and axe appeared before the Great Being. He asked, "Has any one a job to be done for a wage?" The Great Being saw him and asked him,

"What work do you do?"

"There is no art that I do not know. If any one has a house or a pavilion to be erected, I know how it should be built for him."

"If that be so, I have a job."

"What is it?"

"I have invited a hundred thousand crores of monks for the morrow; will you make a pavilion for them to sit in?"

"I will certainly build it for you if you are able to pay me."

"Friend, that I will be able to do."

"Very well, I will build it," said he and went and inspected a site. There was a region twelve or thirteen *yojanas* in extent which was as even as a circlar range used for *kasiṇa* meditation. He gazed on that spot thinking to himself, "Let a pavilion made of the seven precious things rise here covering this space." Instantaneously, a pavilion emerged breaking its way through the earth. On its golden pillars were silver capitals, on silver pillars golden capitals, on jewelled pillars coral capitals, on coral pillars were capitals of jewels and on pillars of the seven precious things were capitals of the same materials. Then he gazed upon it saying, "Let festoons of jingling bells hang down at intervals in the pavilion." Along with his gaze there hung down the festoons, which when wafted by the gentle breeze produced sweet music like that of the fivefold orchestra or as when heavenly music was played. Again he thought, "Let perfumed floral garlands hang down at intervals," and garlands hung down. [**33**] He further thought, "Let seats and supports for a hundred thousand crores of monks emerge, breaking their way through the earth," and immediately they appeared. He next thought,"Let water vessels appear at each corner," and they arose. Having created all this he went to the brahman and said, "Come Sir, look at your pavilion and pay me my wages." The Great Being went and looked at the hall. With one look his whole body became pervaded for all time with the fivefold joy.

And as he looked at the pavilion he thought, "This pavilion is not the creation of a human being. Assuredly, the abode of Sakka has been heated as a result of my intentions and virtue, and hence it could be the handiwork of Sakka the king of the deities. It is not right that I should give alms in a pavilion such as this but for one day, I will give alms for one week." However much an external gift may amount to, it fails to give satisfaction to Bodhisattas, but there arises satisfaction to Bodhisattas from their generosity when they sever their adorned head, pluck out their collyrium-painted eyes, and tear away the flesh from their heart and give them away. Even the generosity of our Bodhisatta, when he was born as Sivi [Jātaka No. 499] and gave alms in the middle of his city within its four gates spending five *ammaṇas*[1] of *kahāpaṇa*s daily, was incapable of producing the satisfaction arising from liberality. But when Sakka, the king of the deities came disguised as a brahman and begged for his eyes, then alone did joy arise in him as he plucked them out and gave them to him. No remorse, not to the extent of a hair's tip did arise in him. Thus there is no satiety accruing to Bodihisattas from generosity. Therefore that Great Being thought that he should give alms for seven days to the hundred thousand crores of monks; he seated them in that pavilion and for a week gave them the alms called Gavapāna. A food prepared with milk boiled to a thick paste over the hearth in large vessels filled with milk, to which are added a little rice, heated honey, powdered palm-sugar, and clarified butter, is called Gavapāna. Men alone were not able to wait on them, but the deities also mingled with them and served them. The space of twelve or thirteen *yojanas* was not sufficient to accommodate the monks, but those monks seated themselves each one by his own powers. On the concluding day he had the bowls of all the monks washed, and he filled them with clarified and fresh butter, honey, treacle, and other articles to be used as medicaments, and handed them back to them together with the three robes. The cloth for robes received by the most junior monk was worth a hundred thousand. While the Teacher conferred his thanksgiving he investigated thus. "This man has given such magnificent alms, what will he be in his future becoming?" He foresaw that he would become the Buddha named Gotama two *asaṅkheyyas* and a hundred thousand æons from then, in the future, and addressed the Great Being, [**34**] prophesying that he would become the Buddha named Gotama after the elapse of such and such a period. The Great Being who listened to the prediction, reflected, "And so I will become a Buddha! Of what use is household life to me? I will seek ordination." Giving up all that prosperity, treating it as a mere blob of spittle, he received ordination under the Teacher; and studying the word of the Buddha he evolved intuitive knowledge and the attainments, and at the end of his life span was born in the Brahmā world.

---

[1]Sinhalese *amuṇa*, a dry measure reckoned as 16 *kuruṇi* (approx. 4 bushels).

The city of the Blessed One Maṅgala was called Uttara. His father was the Khattiya Uttara, his mother Uttarā, his two chief disciples Sudeva and Dhammasena, his attendant monk Pālita, his two leading women disciples Sīvalī and Asokā, his Bodhi the Ironwood tree; and his body was eighty cubits high. When he passed away in Nibbāna, having remained on earth for ninety thousand years, all the ten thousand world spheres became a mass of darkness at one blow. There was great weeping and lamentation among the inhabitants of all the world spheres.

225. Following Koṇḍañña was the Leader called Maṅgala who held aloft the torch of the Dhamma, having dispelled the darkness in the world.

Sumana: Atula

Subsequent to that Blessed One, who passed away in Nibbāna, thus shrouding in darkness the ten thousand world systems, the Teacher named Sumana appeared in this world. He too had three assemblies of disciples: at the first there were a hundred thousand crores of monks, at the second were ninety thousand crores on the Golden Mountain, and at the third, eighty thousand crores. At that time the Great Being was the *nāga* king Atula of great supernatural power and majesty. When he heard that the Buddha had appeared he set out from the *nāga* realm surrounded by his host of kinsmen, and made offerings of celestial music to the Blessed One, who was attended by a hundred thousand crores of monks; he gave ample alms, presenting each monk with a pair of garments, and established himself in the Refuges. That Teacher too prophesied that he would become a Buddha in the future. The city of that Blessed One was called Khema, the king named Sudatta was his father, his mother was Sirimā, his chief disciples Saraṇa and Bhāvitatta, his attendant monk Udena, his leading women disciples Sonā and Upasonā, and his Bodhi the Ironwood tree. His body was ninety cubits in height, and his life span was ninety thousand years.

226. Following Maṅgala was the Leader called Sumana who was unparalleled in all phenomena and the noblest among all beings. [**35**]

Revata : Atideva

Subsequent to him the Teacher named Revata appeared. He too had three assemblies of disciples; the number at the first was beyond reckoning, at the second there were a hundred thousand crores of monks, and a similar number at the third. At that time the Bodhisatta was born as the brahman Atideva; he listened to a discourse of the Teacher, and having established himself in the Refuges, with his hands clasped above his head he extolled the Teacher's conquest of the defilements and made him an offering of his upper garment. He too prophesied that he would become a Buddha. The city of that Blessed One was called Dhaññavatī, his father was the Khattiya Vipula, and his mother was named Vipulā, his chief disciples were Varuṇa and Brahmadeva, his attendant monk Sambhava, his leading women disciples Bhaddā and Subhaddā, and his Bodhi was the ironwood tree. His body was eighty cubits in height and his life span sixty thousand years.

227. Following Sumana was the Leader named Revata who was the highest Conqueror, incomparable, unique, and unparalleled.

Sobhita : Ajita

Subsequent to him there appeared the Teacher named Sobhita. He too had three assemblies of disciples: at the first there were a hundred crores of monks, at the second ninety crores, and at the third eighty crores. The Bodhisatta at that time was born as the brahman Ajita; he listened to a discourse of the Teacher, and having established himself in the refuges gave ample alms to the Brotherhood of monks with the Buddha at its head. He too prophesied that he would become a Buddha. The city of that Blessed One was Sudhamma, his father the king Sudhamma, his mother was Sudhammā, his chief disciples were Asama and Sunetta, his attendant monk Anoma, his leading women disciples Nakulā and Sujātā, and his Bodhi the ironwood tree. His body was fifty-eight cubits in height, and his life span was ninety thousand years.

228. Following Revata was the Leader named Sobhita, composed and of tranquilled mind, unique and unrivalled.

Anomadassi: The *Yakkha* General

Subsequent to him, after the elapse of one *asaṅkheyya*, three Buddhas called Anomadassī, Paduma, and Nārada appeared in one and the same æon. The Blessed One Anomadassī had three assemblies of disciples: at the first there were eight hundred thousand monks, at the second, seven hundred thousand, and at the third six hundred thousand. At that time the Bodhisatta was born as a general of the *yakkhas*, of great supernatural power and majesty, [**36**] the commander of many hundred thousand crores of *yakkhas*. When he heard that the Buddha had appeared he came forth and gave magnificent alms to the Brotherhood of monks at whose head was the Buddha. And the Teacher prophesied that he would become a Buddha in the future. The city of the Blessed One Anomadassī was called Candavatī, his father was the king Yasavā, mother Yasodhara, his chief disciples Nisabha and Anoma, his attendant monk Varuṇa, his leading women disciples Sundarī and Sumanā, and his Bodhi the Terminalia Arjuna.[1] His body was fifty-eight cubits in height and his life span a hundred thousand years.

229. Following Sobhita was the Enlighted One Anomadassī, the chief of men, of infinite fame, glorious, and unsurpassed.

Paduma: The Lion

Subsequent to him there appeared the Teacher named Paduma. He too had three assemblies: at the first there were a hundred thousand crores of monks, at the second, three hundred thousand, and at the third, two hundred thousand monks who dwelt in the dense jungle of the forest far away from villages. At that time when the Tathāgata was living in that thick forest, the Bodhisatta was born as a lion, and kindled great devotion at heart on seeing the Teacher, who had attained to the jhānic meditation of cessation. He saluted him, walked round him with reverence, roared the lion's roar thrice in his joy, and stood there waiting on the Tathāgata for seven days without laying aside his joy, which had thoughts of the Buddha as its basis; and spending his time in joy and ease he sacrificed his life refusing to go in search of prey. The Teacher rose from his meditation on cessation after the elapse of seven

---

[1] The *Arjuna* or *Kakudha* tree, which usually grows near water and is known as *kumbuk* in Sinhalese.

days, saw the lion, and willed that the Brotherhood of monks should come so that he [the lion] would worship them with devotion at heart. Forthwith the monks came and the lion conceived in his mind faith in the Brotherhood. The Teacher read his thoughts and prophesied that he would become Buddha in the future. The city of the Blessed One Paduma was called Campaka, his father was the king Asama, his mother Asamā, his chief disciples were Sāla and Upasāla, his attendant monk Varuṇa, his leading women disciples Rāmā and Surāmā, and his Bodhi the Sona[1] tree. His body was fifty-eight cubits in height and his life span a hundred thousand years.

230. Following Anomadassī was the Enlightened One named Paduma, the chief of men, unique and unrivalled.

Nārada : The Ascetic

Subsequent to him the Teacher named Nārada appeared. He too had three assemblies of disciples: at the first there were a hundred thousand crores of monks, [37] at the second ninety thousand crores, and at the third eighty thousand crores. At that time the Bodhisatta had renounced household life as an ascetic and mastered the fivefold intuitive knowledge and the eightfold attainments; he gave ample alms to the Brotherhood of monks at whose head was the Buddha, and made an offering of red sandalwood. He too prophesied that he would become a Buddha in the future. The city of that Blessed One was called Dhaññavatī, his father the Khattiya Sudeva, his mother Anomā, his chief disciples Bhaddasāla and Jitamitta, his attendant monk Vāseṭṭha, his leading women disciples Uttarā and Phaggunī, and his Bodhi the Great Sona tree. His body was eighty-four cubits in height and his life span ninety thousand years.

231. Following Paduma was the Enlightened One named Nārada, the chief of men, unique, and unrivalled.

Padumuttara : Jaṭila

Subsequent to the Buddha Nārada, during an æon a hundred thousand æons prior to now, there appeared only one Buddha, called

[1] Sanskrit *śyonaka*, *Oroxylumindicum*.

Padumuttara. He too had three assemblies of disciples: at the first there were a hundred thousand crores of monks, at the second ninety thousand crores on the mountain Vebhāra, and at the third eighty thousand crores. At that time the Bodhisatta was born as a district chieftain named Jaṭila; he made gifts of the triple robes[1] to the Brotherhood with the Buddha at its head. He too prophesied that he would become a Buddha in the future. At the time of the Blessed One Padumuttara there were no heretical teachers, so that all the deities and men sought the refuge of the Buddha alone. His city was called Haṃsavatī, his father was the Khattiya Ānanda, his mother Sujātā, his chief disciples were Devala and Sujāta, his attendant monk Sumana, his leading women disciples Amitā and Asamā, and his Bodhi the Sāla tree. His body was eighty-eight cubits in height. His bodily radiance spread around twelve *yojanas* and his life span was a hundred thousand years.

232. Following Nārada was the Enlightened One Padumuttara, the chief of men, the Conqueror, unperturbed like the great ocean.

Sumedha: Uttara

Subsequent to him, when thirty thousand æons had elapsed, two Buddhas named Sumedha and Sujāta appeared in one and the same æon. Even Sumedha had three assemblies of disciples: at the first there were a hundred crores of arahants in the city of Sudassana, at the second ninety crores, and at the third eighty crores. At that time the Bodhisatta was born as a brahman youth named Uttara; [**38**] he gave ample alms to the Brotherhood with the Buddha at its head, spending eighty crores from his wealth, which he had kept deposited in safety. Having listened to the Doctrine and established himself in the Refuges, he went forth from home and became ordained. He too predicted that he would become a Buddha in the future. The city of the Blessed One Sumedha was called Sudassana, his father the king Sudatta, his mother Sudattā, his two chief disciples Saraṇa and Sabbakāma, his attendant monk Sagara, his leading women disciples Rāmā and Surāmā, and his Bodhi the Great Kadamba[2] tree. His body was eighty-eight cubits in height and his life span ninety thousand years.

---

[1]Read *ticīvaradānaṃ* as with SHB.

[2]*Nauclea cadamba*, Sinhalese *kolon*.

233. Following Padumuttara was the Leader named Sumedha, the sage, unassailable, of immense glory, the foremost in the whole world.

Sujāta: The Universal Monarch

Subsequent to him there appeared the Teacher named Sujāta. He too had three assemblies of disciples: at the first there were sixty thousand monks, at the second fifty thousand, and at the third forty thousand. At that time the Bodhisatta was born as a Universal Monarch, and came to him when he heard that the Buddha had appeared; listening to the Doctrine, he dedicated the rulership of the four great continents together with the seven Treasures to the Brotherhood with the Buddha at its head, and received ordination under the Teacher. All the inhabitants of the country, working for the mainstay of the monasteries took with them the produce of the land and continually gave alms generously to the Brotherhood at whose head was the Buddha. This Teacher too prophesied about him. The city of that Blessed One was called Sumaṅgala, his father was the king named Uggata, his mother Pabhāvatī, the chief disciples were Sudassana and Deva, his attendant monk Nārada, the leading women disciples were Nāgā and Nāgasamālā, and his Bodhi was the Giant Bamboo. It is said that this tree was less hollow and had a thicker stem than ordinary bamboos, and with its large branches above, shone like a cluster of peacock feathers. The body of that Blessed One was fifty cubits in height and his life span was ninety thousand years.

234. Within the same Maṇḍa-æon appeared the Leader called Sujāta, lion jawed, of taurine chest, incomparable, and unassailable.

Piyadassī: Kassapa

Subsequent to him, eighteen hundred æons prior to now, three Buddhas named Piyadassī, Atthadassī, and Dhammadassī appeared in one and the same æon. Piyadassī too had three assemblies of disciples: at the first there were a hundred thousand crores of monks, at the second, ninety crores, and at the third eighty crores. At that time the Bodhisatta was born as the brahman youth Kassapa and had reached proficiency in the three Vedas; he listened to a discourse of the Teacher, built a monastery donating riches worth a hundred thousand crores, [**39**] and established himself in the Refuges and Precepts. Then the Teacher prophesied that he would become a Buddha eighteen hundred æons afterwards. The city of that Blessed One was called Anoma, his father the king Sudinna, his mother Candā, his chief disciples were Pālita and Sabbadassī, his attendant monk Sobhita, his leading women disciples Sujātā and Dhammadinnā, and his Bodhi the Piyaṅgu tree.[1] His body was eighty cubits in height and his life span ninety thousand years.

235. Following Sujāta was the leader of the world Piyadassī, the self-evolved, unassailable, unique, and of great glory.

Atthadassī: Susīma

Subsequent to him there appeared the Teacher called Atthadassī. He too had three assemblies of disciples: there were nine million eight hundred thousand monks at the first, at the second eight million eight hundred thousand, and a similar number at the third. At that time the Bodhisatta was born as an ascetic of great psychic power named Susīma; he brought a canopy of Mandārava flowers from the deva world and offered it to the Teacher. He too prophesied that he would become a Buddha in the future. The city of that Blessed One was called Sobhita, his father the king Sāgara, his mother Sudassanā, his chief disciples Santa and Upasanta, his attendant monk Abhaya, his leading women disciples Dhammā and Sudhammā, and his Bodhi the Campaka tree. His body was eighty cubits in height. The bodily radiance remained all the time pervading a region of a *yojana*'s extent all round. His life span was a hundred thousand years.

236. Within the same Maṇḍa æon, Atthadassī the hero among men attained the highest Enlightenment, destroying the great darkness.

Dhammadassī: Sakka

Subsequent to him there appeared the Teacher named Dhammadassī. He too had three assemblies of disciples: at the first there were a hundred crores of monks, at the second seventy crores, and at the third eighty crores. At that time the Bodhisatta was born as Sakka the king of the deities; he made offerings of divine perfumes and flowers and

---

[1] *Piyaṅgu* is a small plant. Its seed is used as an emetic. The reference here probably is to the Piyaka tree, a variety of *kadamba,* Bv has *kakudha* (*Terminalia arjuna*).

heavenly music. He too prophesied about him. The city of that Blessed One was called Saraṇa, his father the king Saraṇa, his mother Sunandā, his chief disciples were Paduma and Phussadeva, his attendant monk Sunetta, his leading women disciples Khemā and Sabbanāmā, and his Bodhi the Red Amaranth tree whose other name is Bimbijāla. His body was eighty cubits in height and his life span a hundred thousand years.

237. Within the same Maṇḍa æon, Dhammadassī of great fame illuminated the world with its deities, having dispelled the impenetrable darkness. [**40**]

Siddhattha: Maṅgala

Subsequent to him, during the æon ninety-four æons prior to now, there appeared but one Buddha who was named Siddhattha. He too had three assemblies of disciples: at the first there were a hundred thousand crores of monks, at the second ninety crores, and at the third eighty crores. At that time the Bodhisatta was born as an ascetic named Maṅgala, of immense supernatural power and endowed with the powers of intuitive knowledge; he brought a large rose-apple fruit and gave it to the Tathāgata. The Teacher partook of that fruit and prophesied to the Bodhisatta that he would become a Buddha ninety-four æons later. The city of that Blessed One was called Vebhara, his father the king Jayasena, his mother Suphassā, his chief disciples, Sambahula and Sumitta, his attendant monk Revata, his leading women disciples Sīvalī and Surāmā, and his Bodhi the Kaṇikāra[1] tree. His body was sixty cubits in height and his life span a hundred thousand years.

238. Following Dhammadassī the Leader called Siddhattha destroyed all darkness like the sun that has risen in the sky.

Tissa: Sujāta

Subsequent to him ninety-two æons prior to now, two Buddhas named Tissa and Phussa appeared in one and the same æon. The Blessed One Tissa had three assemblies of disciples: at the first there were a hundred crores of monks, at the second ninety crores, and at the

---

[1] *Cochlospermum religiosum*, Sinhalese *kiṇihiri*.

third eighty crores. At that time the Bodhisatta was born as the Khattiya called Sujāta possessing great wealth and fame; he renounced the household life taking to an ascetic life, and attained great psychic powers. Having heard that the Buddha had appeared he brought divine Mandārava blossoms and Pāricchattaka flowers and offered them to the Tathagata, who was moving amidst the fourfold assembly; and he made a canopy of flowers in the sky. The Teacher too prophesied that he would become a Buddha ninety-two æons later. The city of that Blessed One was called Khema, his father the Khattiya Janasandha, his mother Padumā, his chief disciples Brahmadeva annd Udaya, his attendant monk Sambhava, and his leading women disciples Phussā and Sudattā, and his Bodhi the Tomentosa[1] tree. His body was sixty cubits in height and his life span a hundred thousand years.

239. Following Siddhattha was Tissa, who was unique and unrivalled, of infinite virtures and boundless fame, the highest Leader of the world.

Phussa: Vijitāvī

Subsequent to him there appeared the Teacher named Phussa. He too had three assemblies of disciples: at the first there were six million monks, at the second and the third five million and thirty-two hundred thousand respectively. At that time the Bodhisatta was born as the Khattiya Vijatāvī; he gave up his large kingdom, and receiving ordination under the Teacher, [**41**] studied the three Piṭakas, and preached the Doctrine to the great multitude. And he fulfilled the Perfection of Morality. This Buddha too prophesied in like manner. The city of the Blessed One Phussa was Kāsi, his father the king Jayasena, his mother Sirimā, his chief disciples Surakkhita and Dhammasena, his attendant monk Sabhiya, his leading women disciples Cālā and Upacālā, and his Bodhi was the Myrobalan[2] tree. His body was fifty-eight cubits in height and his life span nine hundred thousand years.

240. Within the same Maṇḍa æon was the unique Teacher Phussa, incomparable and unrivalled, the highest Leader of the world.

---

[1]Asana, *Terminalia tomentosa*, Sinhalese *piyā*.

[2]Āmalaka, *Phyllanthus embelica*, Sinhalese *nelli*.

Vipassī: Atula

Subsequent to him, ninety-one æons prior to now there appeared the Blessed One Vipassī. He too had three assemblies of disciples: at the first there were six million eight hundred thousand monks, at the second one hundred thousand, and at the third eighty thousand. At that time the Bodhisatta was born as the *nāga* king Atula of great supernatural power and majesty; he gave the Blessed One a golden stool inlaid with the seven precious gems. He too prophesied that he would become a Buddha ninety-one æons later. The city of that Blessed One was called Bandhumatī, his father the king Bandhumā, his mother Bandhumatī, his chief disciples Khaṇḍa and Tissa, his attendant monk Asoka, his leading women disciples Candā and Candamittā, and his Bodhi the Pāṭali[1] tree. His body was eighty cubits in height, and his bodily radiance remained continually pervading a region of a *yojana*'s extent. His life span was eighty thousand years.

241. Following Phussa, the Enlightened One, the highest of men, the discerning one Vipassī by name, appeared in the world.

Sikhī: Arindama

Subsequent to him, in the thirty-first æon from now in the past, there appeared two Buddhas called Sikhī and Vessabhū. Sikhī too had three assemblies of disciples: at the first there were a hundred thousand monks, at the second eighty thousand, and at the third seventy thousand. At that time the Bodhisatta was born as the king Arindama; he made great offerings including robes to the Brotherhood of monks with the Buddha at its head, and gave a lordly elephant decked with the seven kinds of gems, and also articles permissible for their use heaped to the height of an elephant. He too prophesied that he would become a Buddha thirty-one æons later. The city of that Blessed One was called Aruṇavatī, his father the Khattiya Aruṇa, his mother Pabhāvatī, his chief disciples Abhibhū and Sambhava, his attendant monk Khemaṅkara, his leading women disciples Makhilā and Padumā, and

---

[1]The trumpet flower, *Stereospermum svaveolens*, Sinhalese *palol*.

his Bodhi the Puṇḍarīka tree.[1] [**42**] His body was thiry-seven cubits in height, and his bodily radiance remained pervading a region of three *yojanas*. His life span was thirty-seven thousand years.

242. Following Vipassī was the Enlightened One Sikhī by name, the highest among men, the Conqueror, unique and unrivalled.

Vessabhū : Sudassana

Subsequent to him the Teacher named Vessabhū appeared. He too had three assemblies of disciples: at the first there were eight million monks, at the second seven million, and at the third six million. At that time the Bodhisatta was born as the king Sudassana; he made great offerings including robes to the Brotherhood of monks with the Buddha at its head, and received ordination under him. Being endowed with virtuous conduct he obtained constant joy through his thoughts on the Buddha. That Blessed One too prophesied that he would become a Buddha thirty-one æons later. The city of that Blessed One was called Anupama,[2] his father was the king Suppatīta, his mother Yasavatī, his chief disciples Sona and Uttara, his attendant monk Upasanta, his leading women disciples Dāmā and Samālā, and his Bodhi the Sāla tree. His body was sixty cubits in height, and his life span was sixty thousand years.

243. Within that same Maṇḍa æon the unique and unrivalled Conqueror Vessabhū by name appeared in the world.

Kakusandha : Khema

Subsequent to him, during the present æon there were born four Buddhas, Kakusandha, Koṇagamana, Kassapa, and Our Blessed One. The Blessed One Kakusandha had only one assembly of disciples in which there were forty-thousand monks. At that time the Bodhisatta was born as the king Khema; he made great offerings including bowls and robes to the Brotherhood of monks with the Buddha at its head, and

---

[1]*Puṇḍarīka*, belonging to the mangifera species, is quite different from the usual *puṇḍarīka* which occurs frequently in Pāli, a variety of white water-lily. Cf. Sinhalese *äṭamba*.

[2]As with SHB, Fsb. has Anopama, Bv Anoma.

further gave collyrium and other medicines. Having listened to a discourse of the Teacher he renounced household life. This Teacher too prophesied about him. The city of the Blessed One Kakusandha was called Khema, his father the Brahman Aggidatta, his mother the Brahman-lady Visākhā, his chief disciples Vidhura and Sañjiva, his attendant monk Buddhija, his leading women disciples Sāmā and Campakā, and his Bodhi the great Sirīsa-tree.[1] His body was forty cubits in height and his life span forty thousand years.

244. Following Vessabhū was the Enlightened One named Kakusandha, the foremost among men, incomparable, and unassailable. [**43**]

Koṇāgamana: Pabbata

Subsequent to him there appeared the Teacher Koṇāgamana. He too had only one assembly of disciples at which there were thirty thousand monks. At that time the Bodhisatta was born as the king Pabbata; he visited the Teacher in the company of his band of ministers and listened to a discourse, after which he invited the Brotherhood of monks with the Buddha at its head, and gave sumptuous alms as well as washed silk, soft China silk, Kasi silk, woollen cloth, fine linen, and cloth woven with gold threads; and received ordination under the Teacher. He too prophesied about him. The city of that Blessed One was called Sobhavatī, his father the Brahman Yaññadatta, his mother the brahman lady Uttarā, his chief disciples were Bhīyasa and Uttara, his attendant monk Sotthiya, his leading women disciples Samuddā and Uttarā, and his Bodhi the Fig tree.[2] His body was thirty cubits in height and his life span thirty thousand years.

245. Following Kakusandha was the Enlightened One Koṇāgamana, the foremost among men, the Conqueror, the chief of the world, and hero among men.

---

[1]*Accacia sirissa.*

[2]*Ficus glomerata*, Sinhalese *dimbul.*

Kassapa: Jotipāla

Subsequent to him the Teacher called Kassapa appeared in the world. He too had one assembly of disciples at which there were twenty thousand monks. At that time the Bodhisatta was born as the brahman youth Jotipāla; he had reached perfection in the three Vedas and become famed on earth and in the sky [heavens], and was the friend of the potter Ghaṭīkāra. He visited the Teacher with him and listening to a discourse received ordination; and with great perseverance he studied the three Piṭakas and illuminated the dispensation of the Buddha by his gift for discharging the monastic obligations. This Teacher too prophesied about him. The city where this Blessed One was born was Bārāṇasī, his father was the Brahman Brahmadatta, his mother the brahman lady Dhanvatī, his chief disciples were Tissa and Bhāradvaja, his attendant monk was Sabbamitta, his leading women disciples were Anujā and Uruvelā, and his Bodhi was the Banyan tree. His body was twenty cubits in height and his life span twenty thousand years.

246. After Koṇāgamana was the Enlightened One Kassapa the foremost among men, the Conqueror, the king of the Doctrine of great effulgence.

The Buddhas

During the æon in which Dīpaṅkara the Lord of ten Powers appeared, there were three other Buddhas. The Bodhisatta received no assurance under them; [**44**] therefore they are not mentioned here; but the commentary makes the following statement in order to enumerate all the Buddhas starting from that æon:

247. Taṇhaṅkara, Medhaṅkara, as well as Saraṇaṅkara, the Enlightened One Dīpaṅkara, and Koṇḍañña, the highest among men.
248. Maṅgala, Sumana, and Revata, the Sage Sobhita, Anomadassī, Paduma, Nārada, and Padumuttara,
249. Sumedha and Sujāta and Piyadassī of great fame, Atthadassī, Dhammadassī, and Siddhattha, the Leader of the world,
250. Tissa and Phussa and the Enlightened One Vipassī, Sikhī, Vessabhū, Kakusandha, Koṇāgamana, and the Leader Kassapa —
251. These were the Enlightened Ones, free from attachment, well controlled in mind, who were born like the hundred-rayed sun

dispelling the great darkness. They flamed forth like columns of fire and passed away in Nibbāna along with their disciples.

Herein, our Bodhisatta spent four *asaṅkheyyas* and a hundred thousand æons making his resolutions under twenty-four Buddhas commencing with Dīpaṅkara. No Buddha other than this perfectly Enlightened One appeared after the Blessed One Kassapa. In this manner the Bodhisatta received his assurance under the twenty-four Buddhas beginning with Dipaṅkara. For it is said:

> The resolution which consists of a combination of the eight conditions — birth as a human being, the advantage of sex, the good fortune, the meeting with a Teacher, ordination, endowment of latent capabilities to higher knowledge, the dedication of one's life, and resolute will — reaches its fulfilment.[1]

As a result of the resolution, "Well then, let me seek here and there the contributory conditions to Enlightenment"[2] made at the feet of Dīpaṅkara, by bringing together these eight conditions, he summoned all courage and saw the contributory conditions to Enlightenment, commencing with the Perfection of Generosity [when he said,] "Whilst investigating them I perceived the first Perfection of Generosity,"[3] and fulfilling them he reached his birth as Vessantara. And as he thus progressed, all those advantages accruing to Bodhisattas who have made their resolution are thus extolled.

252. Thus those beings who are endowed with all the factors and are assured of their Enlightenment during their long sojourn in the cycle of becoming consisting of many hundreds of crores of æons,
253. Are not born in Avīci nor in the Lokantarika hells, nor are they subject to the hunger and thirst in births as departed beings who are consumed by fire and given to constant hankering, nor born as evil spirits in constant want.[4] **[45]**
254. Though born in the evil state as animals they do not become tiny creatures. When born among men, they are never born blind.

---

[1]Verse 69 (above, p. 18).

[2]Verse 125 (above, p. 25).

[3]Verse 126 (above, p. 25).

[4]The numbering and arrangement of verses from here differs from Fsb.

255. They will not be deficient in hearing, nor will they be dumb nor paralytic. They will not be born as women, nor in the categories of hermaphrodites and eunuchs.
256. Those men who are assured of their Enlightenment are not thus overwhelmed. They are delivered of the heinous crimes; and their conduct is pure in all spheres.
257. They do not recourse to perverse views, and they have an insight into action and activity.[1] Though they dwell in the heavens they will not be born in non-conscious states.
258. There is no cause for them to be born in the Pure Abodes.[2] Bent on renunciation, these virtuous men who are detached from reiterated existence wander forth for the well-being of the world, fulfilling all their Perfections.

The Perfection of Generosity

He came along [in Saṃsāra] having gained those advantages. While he was fulfilling the Perfections there was no limit to the various existences during which he developed the Perfection of Generosity; such as during the times when he was born as the brahman Akitti, the brahman Saṅkha, the kings Dhanañjaya, Mahāsudassana, Mahāgovinda, the great Nimi, the prince Canda, the merchant prince Visayha, the king Sivi, and as Vessantara. So indeed it is said of him in the Birth Story of the Wise Hare [Jātaka No. 316]:

259. Seeing him coming begging for food I sacrificed my own self. There is none to equal me in charity — this is my Perfection of Generosity.

The Perfection of Morality

As he thus sacrificed himself his Perfection of Generosity turned into its Supreme Perfection. Similarly, there is no limit to the various existences during which he fulfilled the Perfection of Morality; such as in the times when he was born as the *nāga* kings Sīlavā, Campeyya, Bhūridatta, and Chaddanta, and as the prince Alīnasattu, son of king

---

[1]They are not nihilists (*natthikavādī*) but acknowledge the working of karma.

[2]*Suddhāvāsa*: they are, Avihā, Atappā, Sudassā, Sudassī, and Akaniṭṭha.

Jayaddisa. So indeed it is said of him in the Birth Story of Saṅkhapāla [Jātaka No. 524]:

260. I was not annoyed with the village lads even while they pricked me with stakes and hacked me with weapons — this is my Perfection of Morality.

The Perfection of Renunciation

As he thus sacrified himself, his Perfection of Morality turned into its Supreme Perfection. Similarly, there is no limit to the various existences during which he fulfilled the Perfection of Renunciation; such as in the times when he was born as the prince Somanassa, the prince Hatthipāla, and the Wise Ayoghara and gave up his kingdom. So indeed it is said of him in the Birth-Story of Cūlasutasoma [Jātaka No. 525]: [**46**]

261. I gave up, like a blob of spittle, the kingdom which came into my possession. As I gave it up I had no attachment for it, and this is my Perfection of Renunciation.

The Perfection of Wisdom

As he thus departed leaving behind his kingdom, being free from clinging, his Perfection of Renunciation turned into its Supreme Perfection. Similarly, there is no limit to the various existences during which he fulfilled the Perfection of Wisdom; such as in the times when he was born as the Wise Vidhura, the Wise Mahāgovinda, the Wise Kuddāla, the Wise Araka, the wandering ascetic Bodhi, and the Wise Mahosadha. So indeed it is said of him when he was born as the Wise Senaka in the Birth-Story of the Bag of Flour-cake (Sattubhasta) [Jātaka No. 240]:

262. Investigating with my wisdom, I relieved the brahman of his pain. There is none to equal me in wisdom, and this is my Perfection of Wisdom.

The Perfection of Effort

As he pointed out the serpent that had crept into the bag his Perfection of Wisdom turned into its Supreme Perfection. Similarly, there is no limit to the various existences during which he fulfilled the Perfection of Effort and others. So indeed it is said of him in the Birth Story of Mahājanaka [Jātaka No. 539]:

263. All the men perished amidst the ocean with no shore in sight; but there was nothing contrary in my way of thinking, and this is my Perfection of Effort.

The Perfection of Patience

As he crossed the great ocean in this manner his Perfection of Effort turned into its Supreme Perfection. In the Birth Story of Khantivāda [Jātaka No. 313]:

264. I showed no anger to the king of Kāsi when he attacked me with a sharp axe as though I was an inanimate thing; this is my Perfection of Patience.

The Perfection of Truth

As he thus endured that great pain while remaining like an inanimate object, his Perfection of Patience turned into its Supreme Perfection. In the Birth Story of Mahāsutasoma [Jātaka No. 537]:

265. I freed a hundred warriors, guarding my truthful speech and forsaking my life; this is the Supreme Perfection of Truth.

The Perfection of Resolution

As he thus guarded his truthfulness at the cost of his life, his Perfection of Truth turned into its Supreme Perfection. In the Birth Story of the Dumb Cripple (Mūgapakkha) [Jātaka No. 538]:

266. My mother and father were not hateful to me, nor was great fame, but Omniscience was dear to me. Hence I did undertake this vow. [**47**]

As he thus resolved on his vow forsaking even his life his Perfection of Resolution turned into its Supreme Perfection. In the Birth Story of Ekarāja [Jātaka No. 303]:

267. No one can strike terror in me, nor am I afraid of any one, but I am consolidated in the strength of my amity, and I always take delight in the open forest.[1]

The Perfection of Amity

As he thus extended his friendliness, with no regard even for his life, his Perfection of Amity turned into its Supreme Perfection. In the Birth Story of Lomahaṃsa [Jātaka No. 522]:

268. I make the cemetery my bed, placing as my pillow dead bones. The herdsmen's children gathered round me and teased me in diverse ways.

The Perfection of Equanimity

As he thus remained unshaken in his equanimity while the village children tried to make him miserable or happy by such acts as spitting at him or offering him garlands and perfumes, his Perfection of Equanimity turned into its Supreme Perfection. This is only a brief account. Its full treatment should be followed in the Cariyāpiṭaka. Having thus fulfilled the Perfections, in his existence as Vessantara it is said:

269. This non-sentient earth not knowing either pain or pleasure — even she, by the power of my generosity, trembled seven times.

Thus, having performed such meritorious deeds which caused the earth to tremble, he passed away from there at the end of his life and was born in Tusita heaven. In this manner, the story so far, from the incident at the feet of Dīpaṅkara up to his birth in the City of Tusita should be understood as the Distant Epoch.

---

[1] *Pavana* is explained as the side of a mountain or a woodland.

THE INTERMEDIATE EPOCH

(Avidūre Nidāna)

The Threefold Uproar

It was when the Bodhisatta was living in the City of Tusita that the tumultuous proclamation of the Buddha arose. For, in the world, three tumultuous proclamations take place, namely, that of the æon, of a Buddha, and that of a Universal Monarch. Herein, a class of deities called Lokabyūha (World Array), who belong to the realm of sensuous existence, having come to know that a new æon would dawn on the elapse of another hundred thousand years, go about in the world of men, with their hair loosened and dishevelled, with sorrowful faces, wiping away their tears with their hands, wearing red clothes, and presenting an exceedingly disorderly appearance. They proclaim, "Friends, a hundred thousand years from now there will be the dawn of a new æon. This world will perish. Even the great ocean [48] will become dry. This great earth and the mighty mountain Sineru will be burnt up and will perish. The destruction of the world will extend as far as the realm of Brahmā. Friends, develop love, compassion, sympathy, and equanimity. Friends, cherish mother and father and be respectful towards the elders of the family." This is called the tumultuous proclamation of the æon.

The guardian deities of the world having come to know that a Buddha, an Enlightened One, would appear in the world on the elapse of another thousand years go about proclaiming, "Friends, a thousand years from now a Buddha will appear in the world." This is called the tumultuous proclamation of a Buddha.

The deities themselves having come to know that a Universal Monarch would appear on the elapse of another hundred years go about proclaiming, "Friends, a hundred years from now a Universal Monarch will appear in the world." This is called the tumultuous proclamation of a Universal Monarch.

The Invitation of the Deities

These three tumultuous proclamations are great. The deities of all the ten thousand world spheres having heard, among these three proclamations, the tumultuous proclamation of the Buddha, assemble all together, ascertain the being who will become a Buddha and go to him and beg of him [to do so]. When they request, they do so at the first appearance of the signs. On this occasion all of them, together with the four Guardian Deities, Sakkas, the deities of the Suyāma, Santusita, Paranimmita, and Vasavatti heavens, and the Great Brahmās of each world system assembled in one world and went to the Bodhisatta in the Tusita heaven and begged of him, "Sire, when you were fulfilling the Ten Perfections, you did not do so with a view to attain the state of a Sakka or a Māra, a Brahmā or a Universal Monarch, but you have fulfilled them with the intention of gaining Omniscience in order to save mankind. Now Sire, the moment has come for your Buddhahood. Sir, it is now the time for your Buddhahood."

The Five Great Considerations: (i) The Time

Then the Great Being, even before giving an assurance to the deities looked for the Five Great Considerations which consist of the time, the country, the district, the family, and the mother and her age-limit. Of these he first considered the time, reflecting whether the time was ripe or not. In this respect, if the normal expectation of life exceeds a hundred thousand years, it is not the time. Why? Because, at such a time, birth, decay, and death are not noticed by beings. Besides, the teachings of the Buddhas are never devoid of the threefold characteristics (*anicca*, *dukkha*, and *anattā*). When transiency, ill, and non-ego are preached to them, they will not think it worth listening to and believing in, but question, "What is it that they talk about?" With the result, it will not be understood. In the absence of this [realization] the dispensation will not lead to Salvation. Therefore this is not the time. When the expectation of life is less than a hundred years, then also it is not the time. Why? Because at such time, beings have defilements to an excessive degree; and admonition given to those whose defilements are acute does not serve the purpose of advice, but like a line drawn with a stick on water[1] it soon **[49]** disappears. Therefore this too is not the

---

[1] *Rāji*, a line or a row.

time. But, when the expectation of life is under a hundred thousand years and over a hundred years, that is the proper time. At that time [the span of] life stood at hundred years; hence the Great Being saw that it was the time to seek birth [on earth].

(ii) The Country

Next, considering the country, he looked at the four continents with their surrounding islands and saw that in three of the continents Buddhas are not born, but only in Jambudīpa; thus he beheld the country. Again considering the region, he thought, "Jambudīpa is indeed large, it is ten thousand *yojanas* in extent. In which district are Buddhas born?", and he beheld the Middle Country. The Middle Country is the region described in the Vinaya[1] with the words: "To the East is the township of Kajaṅgala, and beyond it is Mahāsāla, after that on the near side are the frontier districts; in the middle of the South Eastern region is the river Saḷalavatī, beyond it are the frontier districts as far as which the Middle Country extends; to the South is the township of Setakaṇṇika, beyond it are the frontier districts up to which the Middle Country extends; to the West is the brahman village of Thūna, beyond it are the frontier districts up to which the Middle Country extends." It is three hundred *yojanas* in length, two hundred and fifty *yojanas* in breadth, and nine hundred *yojanas* in circumference. It is within this region that Buddhas and Pacceka Buddhas, the chief disciples and other leading disciples, the eighty great disciples, Universal Monarchs and other powerful Khattiya, and brahman householders of great wealth are born. And he came to the decision, "The city of Kapilavatthu is situated here, and I should be born there."

(iii) The Family

Considering the family next he thought, "Buddhas are not born in a Vessa or Sudda family, but are born in either a Khattiya or Brāhmaṇa family, whichever the people consider as superior at the time. At this time Khattiya families are held in greater esteem; I will be born in one, and the king Suddhodhana will be my father"; and foresaw the family.

---

[1]Vin I 197.

(iv) The Mother

Considering the mother next he thought,"The mother of the Buddha is neither wanton nor addicted to drink, she has fulfilled the Perfections for a hundred thousand æons, and her observance of the five moral vows has remained unbroken from birth. And this queen Mahāmāyā is such an one; she will be my mother."

(v) Her Life Span

And further considering how long she will live he saw that it was ten months and seven days.

Conception of the Great Being

Having thus reflected on the fivefold considerations he honoured the deities by assuring them, "Friends, it is now the time for me to become a Buddha"; and dismissing them by asking them to go, he entered the Nandana Gardens in the City of Tusita in the company of the deities of Tusita. In every heaven there is a park called Nandana, and there the deities go about reminding one another of the opportunities one has had in the past for doing good deeds, repeatedly saying, "Passing away from here you go to a better state." [**50**] He too, being thus surrounded by the deities who reminded him of his good deeds as he went about there, passed away and took conception in the womb of the queen Mahāmāyā.

Queen Māyā's Dream

Here follows the story from the beginning which recounts it fully: At that time, it is said, the festival of the asterism of Āsāḷhi was proclaimed in the city of Kapilavatthu. The people were merrymaking at the festival. Queen Mahāmāyā took part from the seventh day prior to the full moon in the festivities which involved no indulgence in spirituous liquors, but were gay with a profusion of garlands and perfumes; she rose early in the morning on the seventh day and bathed herself in scented water, gave great alms spending four hundred thousand [pieces], and partook of delicious food, decked in all her finery, and entered her decorated bedchamber having set her mind firmly upon the *uposatha* [fast] vows. Falling asleep as she lay on the royal couch she dreamt the following dream:

She felt as though the four Guardian Deities of the world lifted her up with the bed, and taking her to the Himalaya mountain, placed her beneath a great Sāla tree seven *yojanas* in height growing on a plateau of red arsenic sixty *yojanas* in extent, and stood on one side. Then their consorts came forth, and taking the queen to the lake Anotatta, bathed her to rid her of her human stains, and clothed her in heavenly garments, anointing her with divine perfumes, and decking her with heavenly flowers. Not far from that place there is a silver mountain and within it is a golden abode. In it they prepared a heavenly couch with its head towards the East and made her lie upon it. Then the Bodhisatta, who in the form of a lordly white elephant was wandering there on the neighbouring golden mountain, descended from it, and climbed the silver mountain; and coming from the northern direction carrying a white lotus in his trunk which has the lustre of a silver chain, trumpeted. Then entering the golden abode he went reverentially round the mother's bed thrice and appeared as though to have entered the womb making an opening on the right side. Thus did he take conception under the descendant asterism of Āsāḷha.

The Soothsayers

The queen woke up on the following day and told the king of her dream. The king summoned sixty-four eminent brahmans and prepared costly seats for them on the floor made ready for the ceremonial occasion, smeared with yellow dung[1] and strewn with *lāja* and other articles;[2] he offered them as they were seated there gold and silver bowls, covered with gold and silver trays and filled with delicious milk rice prepared with clarified butter, honey, and molasses. He delighted them with other gifts such as unbleached cloth and tawny cattle. He then told the brahmans, whose every desire was satisfied, of the dream and asked them what it all meant. The brahmans replied, "Be not

---

[1]Reading *harit' upalittāya* as in SHB.

[2]Puffed grain, or in the phrase, *lajāpacamāni pupphāni*, "flowers with *lajā* as the fifth item". Dalbergia flower, given in *PED*, is improbable. The five items (powdered rice, white mustard, jasmine buds, thistle grass, and puffed grain) are scattered as a sign of welcome.

anxious, great king, a fœtus has formed in your queen's womb; [51] and that too is of a male child and not of a female: a son will be born. If he leads the household life he will become a Universal Monarch, but if he renounces home and takes to the life of a recluse he will become a Buddha who will unfurl the covering in this world."

The Thirty-Two Omens

The moment the Bodhisatta took conception in his mother's womb the entire ten thousand world systems quaked, trembled, and shook violently with one accord. Thirty-two portents made themselves manifest. An unlimited radiance spread in the ten thousand world spheres. And the blind regained their sight as though to behold this wonder. The deaf regained hearing. The dumb spoke to one another. The hunchbacks stood erect. Cripples were able to walk on their feet. Creatures in bondage were released from imprisonment and fetters. The fire in all the hells was extinguished. Hunger and thirst in the realm of the departed was allayed. Fear among beasts vanished. Disease amongst creatures subsided. All beings became affable. Horses neighed gently and so did elephants trumpet. All musical instruments echoed forth their music. Bracelets and other ornaments of human beings resounded even without striking against each other. All the directions became calm. A cool and gentle breeze blew refreshing every one. Rain fell out of season. Water spouted out from the earth and flowed around. Birds gave up their flight in the sky. The rivers stopped flowing. The great ocean turned into sweet water. Everywhere the surface was covered with the five kinds of lotuses. All varieties of flowers bloomed on land and water; flowers that bloom on creepers — all of them bloomed forth. Lotuses on stalks burst out in clusters of seven one upon the other breaking through slabs of rock on dry land. Hanging lotuses appeared in the sky. Showers of flowers came down on every side. Heavenly music resounded in the sky. The entire ten thousand world systems bearing one mass of garlands and fanned vigorously with yak-tail whisks, were impregnated with the fragrance of flowers and incense and attained the highest splendour, like a ball of flowers spun round and released, or like a wreath of garlands tied firmly together, or like a well decorated flower altar.

The Bodhisatta's Mother

When the Bodhisatta had thus taken conception, four deities with swords in hand stood guard from the time of conception over the Bodhisatta and his mother to ward off any danger. No lustful thoughts towards men arose in the Bodhisatta's mother; and she spent the time in great comfort and glory. She was happy and underwent no physical hardship; and the Bodhisatta who lay in her womb [52] was clearly visible like a yellow thread passed through a clear crystal. Since the womb in which a Bodhisatta has lain is like the relic chamber of a shrine, and no other being can lie in it or occupy it, the mother of the Bodhisatta dies seven days after the Bodhisatta's birth and is reborn in the City of Tusita. Unlike other women who give birth before or after the completion of the tenth month, some seated, others lying down, the Bodhisatta's mother cherishes him for ten months in her womb and gives birth to him standing. This is the general rule with the mother of the Bodhisatta.

Her Journey to Devadaha: The Branch of the Sāla Tree

And Queen Mahāmāyā having cherished the Bodhisatta in her womb for ten months, like oil in a vessel, and being in an advanced stage of pregnancy informed King Suddhodana of her desire to visit her parents' home: "Your majesty, I wish to go to Devadaha, the city over which my family reigns." The king consented, saying, "Very well," and had the road from Kapilavatthu to the city of Devadaha made even, and decorated with plantain trees, pots filled with water, and with banners and streamers and the like; and he seated the queen in a golden palanquin, and entrusting a thousand officers with the task of carrying it, sent her away with a large retinue. Now, between the two towns there is a pleasure grove of Sāla trees, called the Lumbinī Park, belonging to the citizens of both towns. At that time all the trees were one mass of blossoming flowers from the root to the topmost branches. In between the branches and among the flowers swarms of bees of five varieties and flocks of birds of many species moved about warbling in sweet tones. The entire Lumbinī Grove was like the Citralatā forest or like the well-arranged banqueting hall of a mighty king. The queen who saw this felt inclined to besport herself in the Sāla grove. The officers bearing the queen entered the park. Having walked up to the foot of the hallowed Sāla tree she wished to take hold of a branch. The branch bent low like the tip of a well-seasoned cane and came within reach of the queen's hand. She stretched out her hand and held it. At that very instant labour pains seized her. Then the people drew a curtain round her and withdrew. As she stood there clinging to the branch of the Sāla-tree she was delivered of her Child.

The Four Great Brahmās

Almost immediately the four Great Brahmās of pure mind drew near with a golden net and received the Bodhisatta in this net; and placing the Child in front of the mother they said, "O queen, be joyful; to you is born a great son." Unlike other beings who are smeared with loathsome impurities when they leave their mother's womb, the Bodhisatta [53] left his mother's womb like a preacher descending from his pulpit or a man descending from a stairway, stretching out his hands and feet, in an erect posture, unsmeared with any impurity arising from the mother's womb, pure and clear and shining like a precious gem placed on a silken cloth.

The Two Streams of Water

Even though this was so, two streams of water came down from the sky to do honour to the Bodhisatta and his mother and allayed the heat in their bodies. Then from the hands of the Brahmās, who remained there having received him in a golden net, the Four Guardian Deities of the world received him on a cloth of antelope skins [sewn together], soft to the touch, and considered suitable for ceremonial occasions. From them the people received him in a cushion of soft cloth.

The Seven Strides

Releasing himself from their hands he stood upon the earth and looked towards the East. Many thousands of world spheres became like a courtyard to him. The deities and men there honoured him with perfumes and garlands and said, "O Great Being, there is no other like you here, how can there be one superior to you?" In this manner he surveyed the ten directions consisting of the four quarters, the four sub-directions, the nadir and the zenith, and without seeing any one to equal him he took seven strides saying, "Here lies the northern direction," while the Great Brahmā held the white parasol above him, Suyāma the yak-tail whisk, and the other deities followed carrying the other insignia of royalty in their hands. Then at the seventh step he stopped and roared the lion's roar proclaiming the victorious utterance beginning with, "I am the chief of the world."

Mahosadha

And the Bodhisatta made a proclamation in three births immediately after leaving his mother's womb: in his birth as Mahosadha, as Vessantara, and in this birth. In his birth as Mahosadha, as he left the mother's womb, Sakka the king of the deities came and placed a piece of sandalwood core in his hand and departed. He held it in his fist and came forth. Then his mother asked:

"What have you brought with you, dear, as you come?"

"A medicine, mother."

On account of the fact that he came into the world bringing with him a medicine they named him Osadha-dāraka (Medicine-child). Taking that medicine they placed it in an earthenware vessel. It alone served as a drug for removing the ailments of all the blind and the deaf and others who came there. On account of the reputation that arose, "Great is this medicine, great is this medicine" he received the name Mahosadha. On the other hand, in his birth as Vessantara, as he left the mother's womb he came forth saying, "Mother, is there anything in the house? I wish to give away in charity." Then his mother took his hand in hers and placed in it a purse containing a thousand saying, "You are born in a rich family, dear." [**54**] And it is said that in this birth he roared this lion's roar. Thus did the Bodhisatta make his proclamation in three births as he left his mother's womb.

The Seven Sahajātas

The thirty-two portents appeared at the time of his birth as on the occasion of his conception. At the same time as our Bodhisatta was born in the Lumbinī Grove, Rāhula's mother the queen, Channa the minister, Kāludāyī the minister, the lordly elephant of high breed, the royal horse Kanthaka, the great Bodhi tree, and the four treasure urns, also came into being. Of these [four] one was a *gāvuta*[1] in size, one half a *yojana*, one three *gāvutas*, and the other a *yojana*. These seven are called the Sahajātas (of simultaneous appearance). The inhabitants of both cities went to Kapilavatthu taking with them the Bodhisatta.

Kāḷadevala

On that very day hosts of deities in Tāvatiṃsa, joyful and delighted that a son was born to the great king Suddhodana of the city of Kapilavatthu and that he would become a Buddha seated at the foot of the Bodhi tree, were rejoicing, waving garments above their heads. At that time the hermit named Kāḷadevala, a frequent visitor to the palace of the great king Suddhodana and master of the eight attainments, had gone to the Tāvatiṃsa abode to spend the noonday heat after his repast; seated there resting himself he saw those deities and asked them, "What is the reason for your great rejoicing and your being so joyful and delighted? Tell me also the reason for it." The deities replied, "Sir, a son is born to king Suddhodana; seated at the foot of the Bodhi tree he will become a Buddha and set rolling the wheel of the Dhamma. The reason why we are glad is that we will get an opportunity to see his infinite Buddha splendour and listen to the doctrine."

He Receives His Father's Homage

The ascetic who heard their words immediately descended from the world of the deities and entered the royal palace; seated in the seat made ready for him he said, "Great King, a son is born to you, they say; I wish to see him." The king had the child brought decked in all splendour, and carried it up to salute the ascetic. The Bodhisatta's feet having turned around planted themselves on the matted locks of the ascetic. For, in that birth there is no one who can receive worship from the Bodhisatta. Had they through ignorance placed the Bodhisatta's head at the feet of the ascetic, his [the latter's] head would have split in seven. The ascetic, who realized that he should not bring about his self-destruction, rose from his seat and clasped his hands in homage to the Bodhisatta. The king who saw this miracle himself paid homage to his son. The ascetic was able to call to mind [events in] eighty æons, forty

---

[1]The distance an ox wagon can cover before the animals are tired. Four *gāvutas* = 1 *yojana*.

in the past and forty in the future. On seeing the characteristic marks of the Bodhisatta he investigated, reflecting whether he would become a Buddha or not; and when he perceived that without doubt he would, he smiled thinking what a wonderful being he was. **[55]** Further, investigating whether he would get an opportunity to see him when he became a Buddha, he perceived that he would not, but that he would die before that time and be born in a formless existence in which he would not be able to receive awakening even while a hundred or a thousand Buddhas appeared. Lamenting the great loss that was to come upon him, he wept. People saw him and asked: "Our master smiled just now, but again he has begun to weep. What is it, Sir? Will any misfortune befall our little master?"

"No misfortune will befall him; he, for certain, will become a Buddha."

"Then why did you weep?"

He said, "I will not get the opportunity to see a person his like when he becomes a Buddha. Great will be my loss. Bewailing my condition I weep."

The Child Nālaka

Then, reflecting whether there was anyone among his kinsmen who would get an opportunity to see him or not when he became a Buddha, he saw his nephew, the child Nālaka. He went to his sister's house and asked: "Where is your son Nālaka?"

"In the house, brother."

"Call him."

He told him as he came to him, "Dear boy, a son is born in the palace of the great king Suddhodana; he is a Buddha-to-be.[1] He will become a Buddha thirty-five years hence. You will get an opportunity to see him. Renounce household life this very day." The child, who was born in a rich family owning eighty-seven crores, thought that his uncle would not urge him on without a purpose and ordered yellow robes and

[1]Lit. "a Buddha seedling".

an earthenware bowl brought from the market-place immediately; and shaving off his hair and beard he donned the yellow robes saying, "My renunciation has him who is the noblest person on earth as its aim"; and clasping his hands with reverence in the direction of the Bodhisatta he worshipped him, falling prostrate; he next placed his bowl in a bag and hanging it on his shoulder entered the Himalaya region and fulfilled the duties of a monk.

He visited the Tathāgata after his attainment of the highest Enlightenment and requested him to preach the Nālaka Discourse;[1] then returning to the Himalayas he reached Arahantship; treading his noble path he lived for seven months longer and standing beside a golden mountain passed away in the element of Nibbāna free from clinging to the material substratum.

The Interpreters of the Marks

On the fifth day they anointed the Bodhisatta saying, "Let us perform the rite of choosing a name"; they sprinkled the royal palace with the four kinds of perfumes[2] and strewed it with five kinds of flowers with *lāja* as the fifth;[3] having had thick milk rice prepared they invited one hundred and eight brahmans who had mastered the three Vedas, and seating them in the king's palace, fed them with the best food, [**56**] and showed them great honour and requested them to examine the signs, asking them what the child would become. Among them,

270. Rāma, Dhaja, Lakkhaṇa and Mantī, Kondañña and Bhoja, Suyāma and Sudatta — these were the eight brahmans adept in the six [Vedaṅgas] who then expounded the science [of reading the signs].

These eight brahmans alone were to interpret the marks. On the day of the conception, the dream too was interpreted by them. Seven of them raised two fingers and explained in a twofold manner: "A person who is

---

[1]Sn 679–723.

[2]Enumerated as *kāla-agulu* (black aloe), *tagara* (*Coronaria pefume*), *hari-candana* (yellow sandalwood), and oil or *turukkha* (?).

[3]See footnote 2 on p. 67 above. There are in fact no flowers here other than jasmine buds.

endowed with these characteristics, will become a Universal Monarch if he leads the household life, but if he renounces the world he will become a Buddha"; and declared the glory and prosperity of a Universal Monarch. The youngest of them all, Koṇḍañña by clan, a brahman still in his youth, examined the perfection of the noble characteristics of the Bodhisatta and prophesied categorically raising one finger only: "There is no reason for him to live amidst the household cares; assuredly he will become a Buddha who unfurls the covering [of this world]." As he had reached his final existence having made previous resolutions he surpassed the other seven in wisdom, and foresaw one path only open to him. Therefore, he raised one finger and prophesied thus: "There is no occasion for one possessed of these characteristics to remain amidst household cares. Without doubt, he will become a Buddha."

The Group of Five

Thereupon those brahmans returned to their homes and addressed their sons: "Dear sons, we are old. We may or may not get the opportunity to meet the great king Suddhodana's son after his attainment of Omniscience. When that prince attains Enlightenment will you seek ordination in his Dispensation?" And the seven of them remained till their span of life was over and followed their destiny. The young brahman Kondañña remained in good health. He heard that the Great Being had become a mendicant friar, having gone forth in the Great Renunciation on reaching the years of discretion, and had taken up his residence[1] at Uruvelā, whither he had gone in due course and made up his mind, saying, "This is a delightful spot, it is indeed suitable for exertion to a clansman in quest of striving" — Kondañña then went to the sons of those brahmans and said: "I have heard that prince Siddhattha has become a mendicant. It is certain that he will become a Buddha. Had your fathers remained alive [in good health] they would have gone forth in renunciation. If you wish to accompany me, come; I will follow him in his renunciation." They were not able to arrive at a unanimous decision. [57] Three of them did not renounce the world. The other four became recluses appointing the brahman Kondañña as

[1]Correct Fsb. p. 56, line 24, *buddhiṃ* to *vuddhiṃ*, and line 28 *upagato* to *upagate* (agreeing with *Mahāsatte* on line 24 in a locative absolute construction), continue the sentence as with SHB.

their leader. All five of them came to be known as the Pañcavaggiya Theras (the Elders of the Group of Five).

The Four Omens

In the meantime, the king asked: "Seeing what will my son renounce the world?"

"The Four Omens."

"What are they?"

"A person struck down with old age, a sick man, a dead body, and a mendicant."

The king said: "From now on let not any one of these come within sight of my son. My son has no need of Buddhahood. I wish to see him reigning with sovereign powers over the four continents with the two thousand islands surrounding them, and holding sway over the vast [ærial] regions, attended by a retinue filling a circumference of thirty-six *yojanas*." Having said this he placed guards at intervals of a *gāvuta*, in order to prevent these four types of individuals coming within the prince's sight. A member from each of the eighty thousand families of kinsmen who foregathered there on that day at the place of the ceremony promised a son each, saying, "Whether he becomes a Buddha or a king we will give a son each. If he were to become a Buddha he will wander forth attended by a retinue of Khattiya monks; and if he were to become a king he will go about followed by a train of Khattiya princes."

The Ploughing Festival

The king, for his part, appointed for the Bodhisatta nurses of great beauty who were free from all faults. The Bodhisatta grew up amidst great comforts attended by an innumerable retinue. Then one day, the king's ploughing festival was to take place. On that day they decorated the whole city like a divine abode. All slaves, servants, and others assembled at the royal palace wearing new garments and adorned with perfumes and garlands. A thousand ploughs were used for the king's work. On that day, eight hundred ploughs less one, together with oxen, reins, and cords were ornamented with silver. But the plough that was to be driven by the king was ornamented with red gold. The horns of the oxen, the reins, and goad were also ornamented with gold. The king who set out with a large retinue took his son along with him.

The King Pays Homage a Second Time

At the place of work there was a rose-apple tree with thick foliage affording pleasant shade. The king had a couch spread for the prince under it, a canopy decorated with golden stars set up above it, and an enclosure of curtains made around it; he placed guards and went to the place of ploughing, decked in all ornaments and followed by his band of ministers. Thereat the king took the golden plough, the ministers the seven hundred and ninety-nine silver ploughs, and the ploughmen the remaining ploughs. They took those ploughs and ploughed in every direction. The king continued to plough from the near side to the far side and back. And here [**58**] was a great display of splendour. The nurses who were seated round the Bodhisatta came out of the enclosure of curtains wishing to witness the success the king met with. The Bodhisatta who saw no one about as he looked around got up in all haste and sat cross-legged and evolved the first *jhāna* (ecstasy arising from meditation) controlling his inward and outward breath. The nurses went about [enjoying themselves with] food and drink, and delayed a while. The shadows of other trees moved away but the shade of this tree remained spreading out in a circle. The nurses, realizing that their young master was alone, lifted the curtain hurriedly and entered within. They saw the Bodhisatta seated cross-legged on the couch, and also that miracle [of the shadow]; they went up to the king and told him, "Your majesty, your son is thus seated. The shadows of all other trees have moved away, but that of the rose-apple tree remains spread out in a circle. The king returned in all haste and saw that miracle and worshipped his son, saying, "This is the second time, dear, I pay homage to you."

The Bodhisatta Displays His Skill in the Arts

Then in due course the Bodhisatta became sixteen years of age. The king built for the Bodhisatta three palaces suitable for the three seasons: one nine storeys high, one seven, and the other five. He also provided forty thousand dancing women. Surrounded by gaily dressed dancing women, the Bodhisatta was like a deity surrounded by bands of heavenly nymphs, being entertained with the music of an all-female orchestra; he lived in these three mansions in rotation with the seasons enjoying immense luxuries. The queen, mother of Rāhula, was his chief consort.

Whilst he was thus enjoying this great prosperity, one day the following talk arose amongst a group of his kinsfolk: "Siddhattha passes his days in the enjoyment of pleasures. He does not learn any of the arts. What will he do if war breaks out?" The king sent for the Bodhisatta and said. "My son, your kinsmen say, 'Siddhattha spends his time in the enjoyment of pleasures without learning any of the arts.' What do you think of it when this [accusation] is made?"

"Sire, it is not necessary for me to learn the arts. Proclaim in the city by beat of drum that I will display my skill in the arts. Seven days hence I will show my skill in the arts to my kinsmen." The king did so. The Bodhisatta assembled such archers as would shoot at their targets during a flash of lightning or split a horse's hair, and in the midst of the assembly displayed to his kinsmen his skill in twelve ways not shared in common with other archers. This should be understood as handed down in the Sarabhaṅga Jātaka (No. 522). Then did his kinsfolk dispel their doubts.

The Four Omens

Then one day the Bodhisatta who wished to go to the pleasure grove ordered the charioteer to harness the chariot. He said, "Very well," and decking a glorious chariot of priceless worth with all the paraphernalia, **[59]** yoked to it four state horses of Sindhu breed, of the colour of the petals of the white water lily, and announced it to the Bodhisatta. The Bodhisatta climbed in the chariot, which resembled a heavenly abode, and set out for the park. The deities thought, "Prince Siddhattha's time for Enlightenment is drawing near; let us show him the Omens," and presented one of the deities in the form of an old man overcome by decay, with decayed teeth, grey hair, bent and broken-down in body, leaning on a staff, and trembling. The Bodhisatta and the charioteer only were able to see him. Thereupon the Bodhisatta asked the charioteer, as is narrated in the Mahāpadāna,[1] "Friend, what kind of

[1] Mahāpadāna Sutta. Dīgha-nikāya, No. 14.

man is he? His hair is not at all like that of others." On hearing the other's reply he said, "Alas, friend, shame on this existence wherein old age makes its appearance to the born!"; and with agitated heart he turned back from there and went up into his mansion. The king asked, "What is the reason for my son to return so soon?"

"At the sight of an old man, your majesty."

The king said, "They have declared that he will renounce the world on seeing an old man. Hence, do not bring ruin upon me. Quickly arrange dramatic performances for my son [to see]. So long as he enjoys pleasures he will not think of renunciation." Saying this he increased the guards and placed them at a distance of half a *yojana* in all the directions.

When the Bodhisatta likewise went to the park on the following day, he beheld a sick man presented by the deities, and having questioned as before, turned back with agitated heart and went up into his mansion. The king too investigated into it and made the same arrangements as stated earlier; and again increased the guards stationing them in an area extending three *gāvutas* all around.

And further, one day when the Bodhisatta was making a similar visit to the park he saw a dead body likewise presented by the deities, and having questioned as before he again turned back with agitated heart and went up into his mansion. And the king investigated into it and made arrangements as mentioned before and further increased the guard, stationing them in an area extending a *yojana* all round.

Once again, one day when the Bodhisatta again went to the park he beheld an ordained monk, well clad and well draped, presented by the deities, and asked his charioteer, "Friend, who is he?" Even though the charioteer was ignorant as to what a monk was or what his distinctive features were as it was not a time when a Buddha had appeared on earth, by the supernatural power of the deities he was prompted to say, "Sire, this is a mendicant friar"; and he extolled the virtues of recluseship. The Bodhisatta, cherishing a desire for renunciation, continued his journey to the park that day. But the Reciters of the Dīgha[-nikāya] say: "He saw the Four Omens on the same day and went [forth]."

The Bodhisatta is Adorned

Then he disported himself in the park during the remaining hours of daylight and bathed in the royal pond; and when the sun had set he sat on the stone slab meant for the use of royalty, wishing to have himself dressed. Then his attendants stood around waiting on him with garments of many colours, with various kinds of many makes of ornaments and garlands, perfumes, and ointments ready at hand. At that instant the seat on which Sakka was seated became warm. [**60**] He investigated, "Who is it that wishes to make me leave this seat?", and saw that it was the time to adorn the Bodhisatta. He addressed Vissakamma, "Friend Vissakamma, this day at midnight Prince Siddhattha will go forth in his Great Renunciation. This is the last time he will adorn himself. Go to the park and deck the Great Being with all divine ornaments." He agreed, saying, "Very well," and instantaneously by his supernatural divine power went up to him in the guise of his own valet; taking from the valet's hand the cloth used for his headdress, he draped it round the Bodhisatta's head. At the very touch of his hand the Bodhisatta knew that he was not a human being but a *devaputta* (divinity). No sooner the turban was draped round his head than did a thousand layers stand upright, taking the form of jewels and precious gems in the crown on his head. As he continued to drape the thousand layers ten times over, ten thousand layers stood upright. The head is but small, but one should not begin to doubt how so many folds of cloth could remain upon it. However, the largest [fold] among them was of the size of the flower of a Sāma[1] creeper, and the others were only of the size of Kutumbaka[2] flowers. The Bodhisatta's head was now like a Kuyyaka[3] flower with its intertwined filaments. When he had been thus decked in all splendour, he mounted his exquisitely decorated royal chariot; the musicians in his retinue were displaying each one his particular skill; the brahmans were honouring him with words of victory and joy; and Sūtas, Māgadhas, and others were singing panegyrics in unison, uttering festive cries.

---

[1]The Ichnocarpus creeper.

[2]*Kutumbaka* — a shrub with tiny flowers.

[3]*Kuyyaka* — a flower with prominent filaments. It blooms in clusters.

Rāhula's Birth

At that time the great king Suddhodana, hearing that the queen, mother of Rāhula, had given birth to a son, sent a message saying "Convey my felicitations to my son." The Bodhisatta on hearing it, said, "An impediment (*rāhula*) has come into being, a bond has arisen." The king, who came to hear of it on enqiring what his son had said, ordered that thenceforth his grandson should be known as Prince Rāhula.

Kisāgotamī

The Bodhisatta, riding in his stately chariot, entered the city in all pomp and glory and dazzling splendour. At that time the Khattiya maiden Kisāgotamī, who had gone up to the terrace of her mansion, beholding the majestic beauty of the Bodhisatta as he paraded the city streets, gave utterance to the following statement of joy, being exceedingly pleased with his appearance:

271. Tranquilled indeed is the mother, tranquilled is the father, and tranquilled is the woman who has a lord like him. [**61**]

The Bodhisatta heard these words and reflected, "She says that by beholding this physical form such as it is, a mother's heart is pacified, a father's, a wife's. But what should first be extinguished for the heart to become pacified?" As his mind was detached from the defilements, it then occurred to him, "When the fires of attachment, hatred, and delusion are extinguished, and the cares of all the defilements such as those arising from arrogance and dogmatic beliefs are allayed, then only is one tranquilled. A worthy saying has she put into my hearing; and I go about seeking Nibbāna. It is meet that this very day I should give up household life, go forth, and become a religious mendicant in order to seek Nibbāna." He then unfastened from his neck a string of pearls worth a hundred thousand and sent it to Kisāgotamī, saying, "Let this go to her as a teacher's fee." And she was delighted with it, thinking that prince Siddhattha had fallen in love with her and had sent her a present.

The Dancing Girls

As for the Bodhisatta, he returned to his mansion in great splendour, ascended it, and lay on his couch of state. Almost immediately, women decked with all manner of ornaments, proficient in dancing and singing and other arts, as enchanting as heavenly maidens, stood around with their diverse musical instruments, and engaged themselves in dancing, singing, and playing their instruments to entertain him. As the Bodhisatta's mind was detached from the defilements he took no delight in the dance and so forth, and fell asleep for a while. And those women themselves lay down to sleep, discarding the musical instruments they held saying, "He, for whose benefit we engage ourselves in dancing and so forth has gone to sleep. Why need we tire ourselves now?" Lamps fed with perfumed oil were burning. As the Bodhisatta woke up and sat cross-legged upon the couch he saw those women who had lain aside their musical instruments and were sleeping, some of them with saliva pouring out of their mouths, some with the bodies wet with saliva, some grinding their teeth, some talking in their sleep, some groaning, some with gaping mouths and some others with their clothes in disorder revealing plainly those parts of the body which should be kept concealed for fear of shame. He saw the disorder in which they were and became all the more detached from sensual pleasures. The large terrace of his mansion, magnificently decorated and resembling the abode of Sakka appeared to him as a charnel ground full of corpses scattered here and there. The three states of existence seemed to him as a house in flames. He made the inspired utterance, "Alas, this is beset with obstacles! Alas, it is constricted!" His mind was greatly drawn towards renunciation.

The Great Renunciation

He rose from his bed, resolving, "It is meet that I go forth in the Great Renunciation this very day," and went up to the door and called out, "Who is there?" **[62]** Channa, who was reclining with his head resting on the threshold, replied, "Sire, it is I, Channa." [He commanded:] "I wish to set out on my Great Renunciation today. Prepare a horse for me." He said, "Very well," and taking the trappings for a horse went to the stable and saw the stately horse Kanthaka standing on a delightful spot beneath a silken canopy with jasmine flowers on it;

and while lamps fed with scented oil were burning he saddled Kanthaka, saying, "This is the very horse I should saddle today." Even while he was being caparisoned the horse knew, "This caparisoning is very elaborate; it is quite unlike that on other days such as that on the visits to the park for pleasure. It may be that my master wishes to set out on his Great Renunciation today." Then, glad at heard, he neighed very loud. The sound of it would have spread through the entire city; but the deities silenced that sound and allowed no one to hear it.

Rāhula

And the Bodhisatta having dismissed Channa, thought of first looking at his son; he rose from where he was seated, and going up to the apartments of Rāhula's mother, opened the door of the bedchamber. At this time a lamp fed with scented oil was burning inside the room. Rāhula's mother was sleeping in her bed strewn with an *ammaṇa* of flowers such as the large jasmine and the Arabian jasmine; and she was resting her hand on her son. Stepping upon the threshold, and standing there, the Bodhisatta looked at him, and thought, "If I remove the queen's hand, and take my son into my arms she will wake up, and that will prevent my journey. I will come back after gaining Enlightenment, and then see him." With these thoughts he descended from the upper storey. The statement made in the Jātaka Commentary that at that time Prince Rāhula was seven days old is not found in the other commentaries. Therefore this version alone should be accepted.

Kanthaka

In this manner the Bodhisatta descended from the upper storey of his mansion; he went near his horse, and said, "My good Kanthaka, today take me across in one night, and I will, with your assistance, become a Buddha, and take across the inhabitants of the world together with the deities." Then he leapt upon Kanthaka's back. Kanthaka was eighteen cubits in length starting from his neck, and was of proportionate height; he was strong, and fleet of foot, all-white as a cleansed chank [shell]. If he were to neigh or kick his heels, its sound would spread through the whole city. For that reason, the deities by their supernatural power muffled the sound of his neighing so that none could hear it, and placed under his hooves, at each step, the palms of their hands. The Bodhisatta, making Channa cling on to the tail, and himself mounted on the middle of the back of the stately horse, [**63**] reached the great gate [of the city] at midnight. At this time the king had so fixed the doors on the gateways that a thousand men were required to open each door, so that the Bodhisatta would not, at any time, be able to open the city gate, and go away. The Bodhisatta was endowed with great physical strength; reckoned in terms of elephants he possessed the strength of a thousand crores of them, and in terms of men that of ten thousand crores. He thought, "If the door does not open by itself, I will now, seated as I am on Kanthaka's back with Channa clinging to the tail, press Kanthaka hard with my thighs, and jump the rampart eighteen cubits high, and depart." Channa too thought, "If the door does not open itself, I will leap over the rampart seating my master upon my shoulder, and keeping Kanthaka under my armpit taking him firmly round his belly with my right hand, and [so] depart." And Kanthaka too thought, "If the door does not open by itself, I will carry my master upward, seated as he is upon my back, with Channa as well clinging to my tail, and [so] leap over the rampart and depart." Had the door not opened by itself, one or other of the three would have accomplished what he had thought of. But the residing deity of the gate opened it.

Māra

At the selfsame moment, Māra came there with the intention of making the Bodhisatta turn back; and remaining in the sky he said, "Friend, do not depart; on the seventh day from today the wheel of empire will manifest itself to you. You will reign over the four great continents with their surrounding islands numbering two thousand. Turn back, O hero."

"Who are you?"

"I am Vasavatti."

"Māra, I know full well of the wheel of empire manifesting itself, but of sovereignty I have no use. I will become a Buddha causing the ten thousand world systems to resound."

Then Māra said, "Whenever a reflexion of lust, hatred, or malice arises in your mind from now on, I will know of it"; and followed him closely like his shadow without going away from his side, waiting for an opportunity to seize him.

The River Anomā

As for the Bodhisatta, he forsook the universal sovereignty which lay within his reach, like a blob of spittle, without any yearning for it; he set out from the city in great glory on the full moon day of Āsāḷhi under the descendant asterism of Āsāḷha; he then wished to look at the city once again. When this thought arose in his mind the great earth revolved like a potter's wheel that had broken loose, as if it were saying, "O Great Being, once you have done what you have accomplished, it does not require you to turn back and gaze." The Bodhisatta stood in front of the city, gazed upon it, and indicated on that spot the site of the shrine commemorating the place where Kanthaka halted; leading Kanthaka in the direction of the route to be taken, [**64**] he set out with great honour and in supreme splendour. At that time, it is said, the deities bore sixty thousand torches ahead, sixty thousand behind and a sixty thousand each on his right and on his left. Other deities carried innumerable torches on the ridge of the universe; still other deities, *nāgas*, *supaṇṇas*, and others followed honouring him with heavenly perfumes, garlands, powders, and incense. The sky was completly overcast with Pāricchattaka and Mandārava flowers, just as it is with heavy showers when thick rain clouds gather. Heavenly music prevailed. On every side resounded six million eight hundred thousand musical instruments, consisting of the eight and the sixty varieties; and it seemed like a time when thunder roared from the depths of the ocean or the ocean rumbled from the heart of Yugandhara. Proceeding with such splendour, the Bodhisatta traversed three kingdoms in one night and arrived at the bank of the river Anomā covering a distance of thirty *yojanas*. Why was the horse not able to go beyond that? It is not that he was not able; for he was capable of traversing from end to end the confines of one universe, as though treading on the rim of a wheel lying on its hub, and then return in time for his morning meal to eat the food prepared for him. But on this occasion his progress was greatly impeded by his having to extricate himself and cut his way through the tangled mass of perfumes and garlands which rose to the height of his flanks as a result of the deities, *nāgas*, and *supaṇṇas*, and others who remained in the sky showering down perfumes and garlands. That was why he covered thirty *yojanas* only. Then the Bodhisatta, halting on the river bank, asked Channa, "What is the name of this river?"

"Sire, it is called Anomā."

Saying, "And *anoma* (not-of-little-consequence) will be our renunciation," he signalled to the horse by pressing it with his heel. The horse sprang forward and stood on the further bank of the river, which was eight *usabhas* in width.

The Shrine of the Crest Gem

The Bodhisatta alighted from horse-back, and standing on the sandy bank which resembled a sheet of silver, addressed Channa: "Channa, my friend, you go back taking with you my ornaments and Kanthaka. I will become a religious mendicant."

"Sire, I too wish to renounce the world."

The Bodhisatta refused him thrice, saying, "It is not meet that you become a religious mendicant now; you go back." Entrusting the ornaments and Kanthaka to him he thought, "These locks of mine do not become a monk. And besides, I see no-one who is fit to cut a Bodhisatta's locks. Therefore, I myself will cut them with my sword." And taking the sword in his right hand, and holding the topknot with the diadem in his left, he cut it off. The stumps of hair that were left on his head were two inches in length and curling to the right. They remained of that length as long as he lived, and the beard too was in keeping with the hair. It was not necessary for him to shave off his hair and beard again. [**65**] The Bodhisatta took his topknot together with the diadem and threw it into the air, saying, "If I am to become a Buddha let it remain in the sky; if not, let it fall to the ground." The topknot, which was plaited with gems, rose to the height of a *yojana* and remained in mid-air. Sakka, the king of the deities, beheld this with his divine eye and received it in a jewel casket the size of a *yojana*, and founded the Cūḷāmaṇi (Crest Gem) Shrine in Tāvatiṃsa heaven.

272. The highest of men cut off his topknot made fragrant with the best of perfumes and threw it into the sky. The thousand-eyed Sakka,

the descendant of Vasu, received it with head bent low in a precious casket of gold.

The Requisites of a Monk

Again the Bodhisatta thought, "These silken garments of mine are not suitable for a monk." Then the Great Brahmā Ghaṭikāra, his erstwhile companion in Kassapa Buddha's time, with his friendship not grown cold during one whole Buddha-period, thought, "Today my friend has gone forth in the Great Renunciation. I will go to him taking with me the requisites of a monk."

273. The three robes, the bowl, the razor, the needle, the girdle together with the water-strainer — these are the eight [requisites] of a monk who is devoted to religious exertion.

Kanthaka

He brought these eight requisites of a monk and gave them to him. The Bodhisatta donned the banner of the Worthy Ones [the yellow robes], and appearing in the garb of the noble life of recluseship dismissed Channa [with the words], "Channa, tell my parents on my behalf, that I am well." Channa saluted the Bodhisatta, went round him reverentially and departed. But Kanthaka who stood nearby listening to the Bodhisatta's conversation with Channa, was unable to endure the grief at the thought that he would no longer be able to see his master. And going out of their sight he died broken hearted and was reborn in Tāvatiṃsa heaven as the deity Kanthaka. At first Channa had only one cause for sorrowing, but with Kanthaka's death he was overcome by a second sorrow, and he returned to the city weeping and lamenting.

Visit to Rājagaha

And the Bodhisatta, who thus became a religious mendicant, spent a week at the mango grove called Anupiya, situated there in that region, enjoying the bliss of renunciation; [**66**] and covering a distance of thirty *yojanas* on foot he reached Rājagaha in one day. He entered the city and went begging alms from door to door. The whole city was thrown into a state of excitement at the very sight of the Bodhisatta as though at the entry of Dhanapālaka to Rājagaha or the entry of the chief of the Asuras to the city of the Devas. The king's officers went before the king and announced, "Your majesty, a person of this description goes his begging round in the city. We do not know who he is, whether a deity, a human being, a *nāga*, or a *supaṇṇa*." Standing on the terrace of his mansion the king espied the Great Being, and overcome with wonder and amazement he commanded his men, "Go, fellows, and ascertain it: if he is a non-human he will disappear on leaving the city, if he is a deity he will go through the air, if he is a *nāga* he will dive into the earth and disappear, and if he is a human being he will partake of the alms he has gathered." As for the Great Being, he collected a mixed meal, and when he knew that it was sufficient for his sustenance he left the city by the gate through which he had entered it; and seating himself with his face towards the East, in the shadow of the mountain Paṇḍava, began to eat his food. Then his intestines began to turn and were about to come out of his mouth. Being disgusted with that loathsome food, the like of which he had not set his eyes upon before, he then began to admonish himself, "Siddhattha, though you have sprung from a family in which food and drink is found in plenty and are accustomed to eating food prepared from perfumed *sāli* rice kept in storage for three years, and with various delicacies, you were wondering when you would be able to collect scraps of food and eat them like the mendicant dressed in robes made of rags whom you had seen. You have gone forth reflecting whether such a time would come to you. And now see what you are doing!" Having thus admonished himself he overcame his disgust and ate his food. The king's officers saw what took place and went back and informed the king of it. Having listened to the words of his emissaries the king set out from his city in all haste, and arriving at the Bodhisatta's presence was so pleased with the composure of his movements that he offered him all prosperity. The Bodhisatta replied, "O Great King, of material wealth or sensual enjoyments I have no need. I have gone forth resolving on the highest Enlightenment." When the king was not able to gain his consent, even though he requested him in many ways, he said at last, "Assuredly you will become a Buddha. After your Enlightenment do visit my kingdom first." This is the story in brief, but the complete account should be followed by reading the Pabbajjā Sutta which begins with the line, "I shall extol the

Renunciation, how the discerning Sage went forth," together with its Commentary.[1]

Austerities

The Bodhisatta, having given the king his assurance, went in due course on his wanderings to Āḷāra Kālāma and Uddaka Rāmaputta, and evolved the attainments; **[67]** but he rejected as inadequate that progress in spiritual development, realising that it was not the path to Enlightenment; and in order to show to the world of men together with its deities his perseverance and endeavour, he repaired to Uruvelā with the intention of engaging himself in his great striving and took up his residence there, saying that indeed it was a delightful spot, and began practising his great exertion.

And those five religious mendicants with Kondañña as their leader came across the Bodhisatta there on their wanderings in quest of alms through villages, townships, and capital cities. And they became his constant companions during the six years he was engaged in his great striving, and they served him attending to various duties such as sweeping the cell and so forth, saying, "Now he will become a Buddha! Now he will become a Buddha!" And the Bodhisatta himself, who was determined to practise austerities in their most extreme form began to subsist on one grain of sesamum or rice a day. He even took to complete fasting. He dissuaded the deities from infusing divine energy through the pores of his skin. Then his body, which was once golden in colour, turned black from the great emaciation it had reached as a result of that fasting. The thirty-two characteristics of a Great Being were obliterated. And one day, overcome by severe pain whilst engaged in the *jhāna* of the suppression of breath, he fell down unconscious at the edge of the cloister. Then some deities said, "The recluse Gotama is dead"; while others said, "This is only a mode of abiding of the Worthy Ones." Those of them there who thought that he was dead went to the great king Suddhodana and announced to him, "Your son is dead."

"Did he die before his Enlightenment or after?"

"He was not able to become a Buddha. He fell down on the scene of his exertions and died."

---

[1] Sn 405–42.

Hearing this the king refused to believe their words, saying, "I do not believe it. Death cannot come upon him before his attainment of Enlightenment."

Why did the king not believe it? Because he had seen the miracles on the day he took him to worship Kāḷadevala and also at the foot of the Jambu tree.

When the Bodhisatta regained his consciouness and stood up, those deities came back and told him, "Great King, your son is well." And the king replied, "I know very well that my son cannot die like that." When the Great Being was practising severe austerities for six years it was to him like a time of intertwining the sky with knots. Realizing that the practice of such austerities was not the path to Enlightenment he went about gathering alms in villages and townships in order to revert to solid food, and he subsisted on it. Then his thirty-two characteristics of a Great Being reappeared in their natural form, and the body regained its golden hue. The monks of the Group of Five (Pañcavaggiya) left the Great Beings, saying, "Even though he has practised severe austerities for six years he has not been able to realize Omniscience. [**68**] How will he be able to do so now that he has begun to take solid food, going about begging alms in the villages? He now leads a life of indulgence, and he has swerved from his exertions. Our expecting spiritual attainments under him is like a man who wishes to bathe thinking of using dew drops. Of what use is he to us?" They took each his begging bowl and robes and went away; covering a distance of eighteen *yojanas*, they entered Isipatana.

Sujātā

And at that time a maiden named Sujātā, born in the family of the householder Senāni of the hamlet of Senāni in Uruvelā, had reached her years of discretion and made a wish at a Banyan tree: "If I marry a member of a family of equal rank and succeed in obtaining a son as my first child, I will make an annual sacrifice to you spending a hundred thousand." Her wish was fulfilled. Wishing to perform the sacrifice on the full-moon day of the month of Vesākha, on the completion of the six years of the Great Being's practice of austerities, she had first of all sent a thousand cows to pasture in a grove of liquorice. She then made five hundred cows drink their milk, and two hundred and fifty theirs. In this manner she brought the number down to the last sixteen, whose milk eight cows were made to drink; and she made the milk go in this rotation in order to obtain its correct thickness, sweetness, and strength. Thinking that she would perform the sacrifice early in the morning on the full-moon day of Vesākha, she rose at early dawn and milked those eight cows. The calves did not go near the cows' udders. The moment new vessels were placed under the udders streams of milk poured into them of their own accord. Seeing this miracle, Sujātā herself took the milk and poured it into a new pot, and with her own hands built a fire and began to boil it. When that milk rice was boiling, large bubbles rose and ran around turning to their right. Not a drop fell outside. Not even a faint smoke rose from the hearth. At that time the four Guardian Deities of the world came there and mounted guard over the fireplace, and the Great Brahmā held his parasol. Sakka brought the pieces of firewood together and kindled the fire. The deities by their divine power, as though they were extracting honey by squeezing out a honeycomb formed on a stick, brought together the beneficial energy of the deities and men of the four great continents and their two thousand surrounding islands and placed it there. At other times the deities infuse energy at each mouthful, but on the day of the Enlightenment and on the day of passing away in Nibbāna they infuse it into the vessel itself.

The Bodhisatta at the Foot of the Tree

Sujātā, [**69**] who saw the numerous wonders that appeared to her on one and the same day, said to Puṇṇā her slave girl, "Dear Puṇṇā, our deity is greatly pleased today. All these days I have not seen a miracle like this. Go with all haste and prepare the seat of the divinity." Saying, "Very well, lady," and obeying her command she hastened to the foot of the tree. Meanwhile the Bodhisatta, who had dreamt the five great dreams that night, arrived at the conclusion, on examining their significance, that without doubt he would become a Buddha that day; and having attended to his bodily ablutions, on the elapse of that night he went early in the morning and sat at the foot of that tree, illuminating the whole tree with his bodily radiance, awaiting the time of setting out for alms. Thereupon the slave girl Puṇṇā, who came there, saw the Bodhisatta seated at the foot of the tree surveying the eastern quarter, and also saw the whole tree turned golden in colour with the radiance issuing forth from his body; and having seen all this she thought, "Today our divinity has descended from the tree and is seated there, methinks, to receive the sacrificial offering in his own hand." Overcome with fervour she ran to Sujātā and told her about it.

The Golden Bowl

On hearing her words Sujātā was delighted in mind; and telling her, "From now on you will be in the station of my eldest daughter," she gave her all the ornaments as became her daughter. Since it is fit that he should receive on the day of his attainment of Enlightenment a golden bowl worth a hundred thousand, she conceived the idea of serving the milk rice in a golden vessel and had a golden bowl worth a hundred thousand brought to her, and wishing to put the milk rice into it, she tilted the vessel in which the food was cooked. All the milk rice rolled out into the bowl like water from a lotus leaf. The bowl was full to the brim with it. She covered the bowl with another golden vessel and wrapped it with a cloth; and having adorned herself with all ornaments she placed that bowl on her head and went in all her splendour to the foot of the Banyan tree. Overcome with great joy on beholding the Bodhisatta, thinking him to be the tree god, she went up to him, bowing in a humble manner from the place where she first espied him, and taking down the bowl from her head she uncovered it; and taking in a golden water pot water perfumed with sweet-smelling flowers she walked up to the Bodhisatta and stood near him. The earthenware vessel given by the Great Brahmā Ghaṭikāra, which had remained with the Bodhisatta so long, disappeared at this moment. Not being able to find the bowl, the Bodhisatta stretched out his right hand and accepted the water offered to him. Sujātā placed in the hand of the Great Being the milk rice together with the bowl which contained it. The Great Being looked at Sujātā. She understood what it meant and worshipped him saying, "Lord, accept what I have offered you and depart wherever you please. Even as my wish **[70]** has been fulfilled may yours as well be fulfilled!" And she went away with no more desire for the golden bowl worth a hundred thousand than for a withered leaf.

The Bowl Goes Upstream

And the Bodhisatta rose from where he was seated and went reverentially round the tree, and taking the bowl with him he proceeded to the bank of the river Nerañjarā. There is a ford of easy access, the bathing place at which many hundred thousands of Bodhisattas go down into the river on the day of their attainment of Enlightenment. Leaving his bowl on its bank he went down into the river and bathed, and donning the banner of the Worthy Ones, the inner robe worn by many hundred thousand Buddhas, he sat down facing the East and ate all the honeyed milk rice which had been prepared without using water, after having divided it up into forty-nine balls of the size of a single-seeded palmyra fruit. That was all the food he had for the forty-nine days of the seven weeks he spent after his Enlightenment at the foot of the Bodhi tree. During this period he took no other food, he did not bathe nor wash his face nor rid himself of waste matter. He spent the time in the bliss of the ecstasy of *jhāna*-meditation, in the bliss of the Path and its Fruits. Having partaken of that milk rice he took the golden bowl and sent it adrift saying, "If I succeed in becoming a Buddha this day, let this bowl go upstream; if not, let it go down with the current." Cutting its way through the current it went to the middle of the river and proceeded against the current for a distance of eighty cubits, keeping to a central course, as fast as a swift horse. And sinking at a whirlpool it went to the abode of the *nāga* king Kāla, and making a clanging noise striking against the bowls used by the three previous Buddhas placed itself as the bottom most among them. The *nāga* king Kāla heard that sound and began to sing songs of praise in many hundred verses, saying, "A Buddha was born yesterday, and again another today." For to him all this interval during which the great earth rose filling the sky to the extent of a *yojana* and three *gāvutas* was like yesterday and today. And the Bodhisatta having spent his noonday rest [in meditation] in the blossoming Sāla grove on the bank of the river, wended his way in the direction of the Bodhi tree at eventide, the time flowers drop off from their stems, along the path which was eight *usabhas* wide and decorated by the deities, like a lion shaking off his drowsiness. *Nāgas*, *yakkhas*, *supaṇṇas*, and others honoured him with heavenly perfumes, flowers, and so forth, playing divine music. The ten thousand world systems were filled alike with perfumes and garlands as well as with shouts of joy.

The Grass-Seller Named Sotthiya

At that time a grass seller named Sotthiya, who was coming from the opposite direction carrying a bundle of grass, offered the Great Being eight handfuls of grass, impressed with his bearing. Taking the grass the Bodhisatta [71] ascended the platform at the foot of the Bodhi tree and stood on the southern side facing the North. At that moment the southern ridge of the universe sank low and appeared to have reached Avīci below. The northern ridge of the universe was raised upward and appeared to have reached the vault of heaven above. The Bodhisatta thought that perhaps it was not the place for the attainment of Enlightenment, and going round in a clockwise direction he went and stood on the western side facing the East. Then the western ridge of the universe sank low and appeared to have reached Avīci below and the eastern ridge rose and appeared to have reached the vault of heaven above. Wherever he stood the mighty earth was bent downward on one side and raised upward on the other like a wheel of a wagon lying on its hub with the edge of its rim trodden on on one side. The Bodhisatta thought that that too perhaps was not the place for the attainment of Enlightenment, and going round in a clockwise direction, he went and stood on the northern side facing the South. Then the northern ridge of the universe sank low and appeared to have reached Avīci below. The southern ridge rose and appeared to have reached the vault of heaven above. The Bodhisatta thought that that too perhaps was not the place for the attainment of Enlightenment and going round in a clockwise direction he went and stood on the eastern side facing the West. The seat of meditation of all Buddhas is on the eastern side, it trembles not and shakes not.

The Seat of Enlightenment

The Great Being, having realised that that was the stable place, never forsaken by any of the Buddhas, the seat for the destruction of the aggregate of defilements, held those blades of grass at their tips and shook them. And immediately there sprang a seat fourteen cubits in extent. And those blades of grass placed themselves in a manner that even the ablest painter or sculptor would not have been able to design. The Bodhisatta with his back to the trunk of the Bodhi tree and facing the East, made the firm resolve, "Let only my skin, sinews, and bones remain, and let the flesh and blood in my body dry up; but not until I attain the supreme Enlightenment will I give up this seat of meditation"; and he sat down cross-legged in his invincible seat, from which he could not be dislodged even if thunderbolts were hurled at him in their hundreds.

Māra's Legions

At that time the *devaputta* Māra, thinking, "Prince Siddhattha wishes to go beyond my control, but I will not give him the opportunity of doing so," went and announced it to his forces and marched forward with them uttering the characteristic battle cry of Māra. Māra's army in battle array was a column twelve *yojanas* long in front of him and twelve *yojanas* each on either flank [to the right and left of him]; behind him it extended as far as the edge of the universe, and upward to the height of nine *yojanas*. As it rent the air with its war cry, **[72]** it was heard like the rumbling of an earthquake progressing from a distance of thousand *yojanas*. Thereupon the *devaputta* Māra mounted on the elephant called Girimekhala, which was a hundred and fifty *yojanas* in height, and armed himself with diverse weapons creating a thousand hands. No two people of the rest of the army of Māra carried the same type of weapon. They came in diverse forms assuming various guises to overwhelm the Great Being.

The Deities Flee

And at this time the deities of the ten thousand world spheres stood around the Great Being singing songs in praise of him. Sakka the king of the deities stood there blowing his conch shell Vijayuttara. And this shell was two thousand cubits in circumference. When it is sounded once by blowing air into it, its blast lasts four months before the sound finally dies down. The *nāga* king Mahākāla stood singing his praises with over a hundred verses. The Great Brahmā stood there bearing the white parasol. When the army of Māra was fast approaching the foot of the Bodhi tree, not one among them was able to remain; they fled in whichever direction they were facing. The *nāga* king Kāḷa dived into the earth and fled to his *nāga* abode Mañjerika, which was five hundred *yojanas* in extent, and lay down covering his face with both hands. Sakka stood at the ridge of the universe dangling his conch shell Vijayuttara on his back, the Great Brahmā left his white parasol on the edge of the universe and went straight to the Brahmā world. Not a single deity was able to remain there. The Great Being sat there all alone. And Māra then said to his followers, "My men, there is no man to equal Siddhattha the son of Suddhodana. We are not equal to the task of giving him battle face to face. Let us attack him from behind." And the Great Being looked at the three sides and saw the whole place deserted as all the deities had fled. And again beholding the forces of Māra swooping down upon him from the North he continued to sit there reflecting thus on the Ten Perfections: "Such a large force makes a great effort and displays much prowess against me, single handed as I am. In this place there is neither my mother, father, brother, nor any other relative. But these Ten Perfections are like retainers whom I have maintained for a long time. Therefore it behoves me to rout this army making the Perfections themselves my shield as well as the weapon of attack."

The Battle with Māra

Then the *devaputta* Māra raised a tornado wishing to drive away Siddhattha with it. Instantaneously such gales rose from the East and other directions [**73**] as would have shattered to bits mountain peaks of the height of half a *yojana*, two *yojanas* or three *yojanas*, or could have uprooted shrubs and trees of the forest, or could have reduced to fragments the villages and townships in the neighbourhood; but by the virtue and majesty of the Great Being they lost their force, and on reaching the Bodhisatta they were not able to shake even the hem of his robe. Wishing to engulf him in water and slay him, he next caused a heavy downpour of rain. By his great miraculous power clouds gathered in their hundreds and thousands, layer upon layer, and poured forth rain. The earth was hollowed out by the violence of the torrential downpour. A great flood came submerging the tree tops of the forest, but it could not moisten his robe even to the extent of the little space on which a dewdrop would fall. Next he raised a shower of rocks. Large mountain peaks came swirling through the air issuing smoke and flames, but on reaching the Bodhisatta they turned into wreaths of heavenly garlands. Next he raised a storm of missiles. Swords, daggers, darts, and other weapons, single edged and double edged, came hurtling through the sky, smoking and flaming; but on reaching the Bodhisatta they turned into heavenly flowers. Next he raised a shower of burning coals; embers of the hue of Kiṃsuka[1] flowers came flying through the sky and were scattered at the feet of the Bodhisatta turning into heavenly flowers. Next he raised a storm of ashes; red hot ashes, glowing like fire came flying through the air, fell at the feet of the Bodhisatta and turned into sandalwood powder. Next he raised a sandstorm; fine particles of sand

[1]*Butea frondosa*, its flower is red. Sinhalese *eramudu*.

came smoking and flaming through the sky, fell at the feet of the Bodhisatta and turned into heavenly flowers. Next he raised a storm of mud; the mud came smoking and flaming through the air, fell at the feet of the Bodhisatta, and turned into heavenly ointments. He next created a gloom which was as thick as when four conditions are found in combination;[1] on reaching the Bodhisatta it disappeared as darkness that vanishes with the oncoming radiance of the sun.

Māra was thus unable to put the Bodhisatta to flight with these nine storms: of wind, rain, rocks, missiles, embers, ashes, sand, mud, and darkness. He ordered his followers, "My men, why do you stand still? Capture this prince or smite him or put him to flight." He himself advanced upon the Bodhisatta, mounted on the back of the elephant Girimekhala armed with a disc-weapon, and cried out, "Rise, Siddhattha, from that seat. It is not meant for you. It goes to me." On hearing his words the Great Being answered, "Māra, you have neither practised the Ten Perfections, the Sub-Perfections, and the Supreme Perfections, nor made the five great sacrifices, nor have you fulfilled the quest of knowledge, the quest of the weal of the world, and the quest of wisdom. This seat is not meant for you. **[74]** I alone have the right to it."

Enraged at this, Māra, being unable to restrain the vehemence of his temper, hurled his discus at the Great Being. But it turned into a canopy of garlands and remained above him while he was reflecting on the Ten Perfections. It is said that this razor-edged disc weapon, when it is hurled with rage at other times, careers along cleaving asunder pillars of solid rock as though they were bamboo shoots, but now it turned into a canopy of garlands and remained there. Others of Māra's army hurled huge masses of rock, thinking that it would make him rise from his seat and take to flight. But even these turned into wreaths of garlands and fell upon the ground, while the Great Being continued to reflect on the Ten Perfections.

---

[1]The four conditions are: the fourteenth day of the dark fortnight (of the waning moon), a thick forest, a dark cloud, and midnight.

The Earth as Witness

The deities who stood at the ridge of the universe continually raised their heads and craning their necks looked out, saying, "Alas, ruined indeed is the handsome physical frame of Prince Siddhattha! What will he do?" Then the Great Being told Māra, as he stood there claiming the throne accruing on the day of their Enlightenment to Bodhisattas who fulfil their Perfections, "Māra, who will testify to your having given away in charity?" Māra stretched forth his hand in the direction of his army saying, "All these are my witnesses." Instantaneously the cry of one accord, "I am witness, I am his witness," coming from the followers of Māra resounded like an earthquake. Then said Māra to the Great Being, "Siddhattha, who will testify to your having given in charity?" The Great Being answered, "You have sentient beings as witnesses to your having given away in charity, but here in this place I have no living being whatever as my witness. Let alone the generosity I have practised in all other existences, let this great and solid earth, non-sentient as it is, be my witness to the seven hundredfold great alms I gave when I was born as Vessantara"; and extricating his right hand from underneath the folds of his robe, he stretched it out towards the earth saying, "Are you or are you not witness to my having given the seven hundredfold alms in my birth as Vessantara?" And the great earth resounded with a hundred, a thousand, or a hundred thousand echoes as though to overwhelm the forces of Māra, and saying as it were, "I was your witness to it then."

Māra's Defeat

Then as the Great Being continued to reflect on the alms he had given as Vessantara, saying to himself, "O Siddhattha, you have given away vast charities and made the highest sacrifice," the elephant Girimekhala which was a hundred and fifty *yojanas* in height went down on its knees. The followers of Māra fled in every direction. No two fled by the same path. They ran in whichever direction that lay before them discarding their head ornaments and the clothes they were wearing.

The Proclamation of Victory

When the heavenly hosts beheld the army of Māra taking to flight, **[75]** the *nāgas* among them sent messengers to the *nāga* realm, the

Suppaṇṇas to their kingdom, the deities to heaven, and the Brahmās to the Brahmā world, saying, "Māra has been defeated, Prince Siddhattha has triumphed, let us honour him at his victory," drew near the Great Being, going up to his Bodhi seat. And they thus advanced [singing]:

274. For this is the victory to the illustrious Buddha, and defeat to Māra the Evil One. So did the hosts of *nāgas* overcome with joy then proclaim at the foot of the Bodhi tree the victory of the Great Sage.
275. For this is the victory to the illustrious Buddha, and defeat to Māra the Evil One. So did the bands of *supaṇṇas* overcome with joy then proclaim at the foot of the Bodhi tree the victory of the Great Sage.
276. For this is the victory to the illustrious Buddha, and defeat to Māra the Evil One. So did the hosts of deities overcome with joy then proclaim at the foot of the Bodhi tree the victory of the Great Sage.
277. For this is the victory to the illustrious Buddha, and defeat to Māra the Evil One. So did the hosts of Brahmās overcome with joy then proclaim at the foot of the Bodhi tree the victory of the Steadfast Sage.

The Great Being Gains Omniscience

The remaining deities of the ten thousand world systems stood there honouring him with garlands, perfumes, and ointments, and singing his praises in diverse ways. While the sun was still shining above, the Great Being thus dispersed Māra's army; being honoured with the offerings in the form of the young leaves from the Bodhi tree falling on his robe, as though with shoots of red coral, he entered into the knowledge of previous existences in the first watch of the night; in the second watch he purified his divine eye; and in the final watch gained an insight into the knowledge of the interdependent causal origins. As he continued to reflect on the nature of the causal antecedents which consist of twelve constituents, in their direct and inverse relations in progressive and regressive evolution, the ten thousand world systems quaked twelve times up to the very limits of the ocean. When the Great Being gained penetrative insight into omniscient knowledge at dawn, making the ten thousand world systems resound, [**76**] the entire ten thousand worlds assumed a festive garb.

The World in Festive Array

The radiance of the banners and streamers hoisted on the eastern ridge of the world sphere spread as far as the western ridge. Similarly, the radiance of the banners and streamers hoisted on the western ridge, the northern ridge, and the southern ridge spread as far as the eastern, southern, and northern ridges respectively. And the radiance of the banners and streamers hoisted on the surface of the earth remained in constant contact with the world of Brahmā, and that of those held aloft in the world of Brahmā penetrated to the surface of the earth. Flowering trees in the ten thousand world spheres blossomed forth. Fruit-bearing trees were weighted down with clusters of fruit. Flowers that bloom on tree trunks, branches, and creepers blossomed in their respective places. Lotuses on stalks sprang in clusters of seven, breaking through rocky surfaces, and were heaped layer upon layer. The ten thousand world systems revolved and remained like a wreath of garlands tossed about or like a well-arranged spread of flowers. The intervening regions of eight thousand *yojanas* between the world spheres which had not been lit before even with the radiance of seven suns shining together became one mass of light. The great ocean eighty-four thousand *yojanas* deep turned into sweet water. Rivers ceased to flow. Those blind from birth were able to see objects, those deaf from birth were able to hear sounds, and those crippled from birth walked on their feet. Bonds and fetters broke loose and fell apart.

The Ecstatic Utterance

Being thus honoured with unlimited glory and splendour, whilst manifold wondrous happenings were taking place, he gained penetrative insight into the knowledge of omniscience and made the ecstatic utterence customary with all Buddhas:

278. Seeking the builder of the house I sped along many births in Saṃsāra but to no avail; ill is birth again and again.
279. O builder of the house, you are seen. Do not build the house again! All your beams are broken, and the ridgepole is shattered. The

mind that has gone beyond things composite has attained the destruction of the cravings.[1] [77]

All the incidents commencing with his departure from the heaven of Tusita and ending with the attainment of Omniscience should be known as the Intermediate Epoch.

---

[1]Dhp 153–54.

THE RECENT EPOCH

(Santike Nidāna)

The Seven Weeks: The First Week

The Recent Epoch is said to be met with in the numerous instances which make reference to his stay in various places, with such statements as "The Blessed One was dwelling at Sāvatthi in the monastery of Anāthapiṇḍika in Jeta's Grove", or "He was dwelling at Vesāli in the Gabled Hall in Mahāvana". Even though it has been so stated, it should, however, be followed from the beginning in the following manner:

It so occurred to the Blessed One even while he was seated there, having made his esctatic utterance: "I pursued my course in Saṃsāra for four *asaṅkheyyas* and a hundred thousand æons in order to gain this throne of victory. It is for the sake of this throne of victory that during this long interval I severed my crowned head from my neck and gave it away, gave away my collyrium-painted eyes, tore out the flesh from my heart and gave it away, and gave away to work as slaves for others such sons as Prince Jāli, such daughters as Kaṇhājinā, and such wives as Princess Maddī. This, my throne of victory, is a unique throne. Whilst seated here all my aspirations have come to pass, and I will not rise from it yet." And he sat there for seven days, entering into many hundred thousand crores of attainments. With reference to it, it has been said, "Therefore the Blessed One sat continuously for seven days experiencing the bliss of emancipation."

The Shrine of the Steadfast Gaze

Some of the deities there began to reflect, "Even this day Siddhattha for certain has a further duty to perform, but he has not given up his attachment to the throne of victory." The teacher knew their reflection, and in order to dispel their doubts rose into the air and performed the miracle of the double. The miracle performed at the seat of the great Bodhi, that performed in the assembly of his kinsmen, or that performed before Pāṭikaputta, all of them were like the miracle of the double performed at the foot of the Gaṇḍamba tree. Having thus dispelled the doubts of the deities with this miracle, the Teacher, who reflected, "It is on this seat that I have attained Omniscience," stood in a somewhat easterly direction towards the North of the throne of victory where he had attained the fruition of the Perfections which he had fulfilled during four *asaṅkheyyas* and a hundred thousand æons. And that spot came to be known as the Shrine of the Steadfast Gaze.

The Shrine of the Jewelled Cloister

Then, creating a cloister between the throne of victory and the place where he had stood, [**78**] he spent seven days pacing up and down that jewelled cloister which lay from East to West. And that spot came to be known as the Shrine of the Jewelled Cloister.

The Shrine of the House of Gems

During the fourth week the deities created a house of gems at a spot to the Northwest of the Bodhi. And he spent seven days there reflecting carefully on the contents of the entire set of treatises in the Abhidhamma Piṭaka with its endless methods of exposition. But the members of the School of Abhidhamma say that the house of gems here does not signify a house built with gems, but is the place where he had cogitated upon the seven books of Abhidhamma. Since both interpretations are applicable here, both explanations should be accepted. Therefore that spot came to be known as the Shrine of the House of Gems.

Māra's Sixteen Lines

Having thus spent four weeks near the Bodhi tree, in the fifth week he repaired to the Ajapāla Banyan tree from the foot of the Bodhi tree. There too he sat cogitating upon the Dhamma and experiencing the bliss of emancipation. At that time the *devaputta* Māra, thought to himself, "All this while I have pursued him, waiting for an opportunity to seize him, but I have discovered no fault in him; he has now gone beyond my control"; and seated on the highway dejected and downcast, he drew sixteen lines on the ground thinking of sixteen things. He drew one line thinking, "I have not fulfilled the Perfection of Generosity as he has; therefore I have not become like him." Similarly, thinking, "I have not fulfilled the Perfections of Morality, Renunciation, Wisdom, Effort,

Patience, Truth, Resolution, Amity, and Equanimity as he has; therefore I have not become like him," he drew [as far as] the tenth line. He drew the eleventh line thinking, "I have not fulfilled, as he has, the Ten Perfections which serve as the basis for the realization of the unique knowledge of the sensory faculties of others, and therefore I have not become like him." Again, thinking, "I have not fulfilled as he has, the Ten Perfections which are the bases for the unparalleled knowledge of inclinations and dispositions, of the attainment of great compassion, of the miracle of the double, of the removal of obstructions, and of omniscience; therefore I have not become like him," he drew [as far as] the sixteenth line. For these reasons he was seated on the highway drawing sixteen lines in that manner.

The Daughters of Māra

At that time Taṇhā, Aratī, and Ragā,[1] the three daughters of Māra, looked for him, saying, "Our father is not to be seen, where could he be now?"; they saw him, dejected as he was, scratching on the ground. Seeing him, they ran to their father and asked, "Father, why are you so sad and downhearted?"

"My dears, this Great Recluse has now passed beyond my control. I have watched for so long, yet have not been able to see an opportunity to seize him. Therefore I am sad and downhearted." **[79]**

"If that be so do not vex yourself. We will bring him under our power and lead him to you."

"No, my dears, no one can bring him under his power. This man is firmly established in his unwavering faith."

"But, dear father, we are women; we will ensnare him in such bonds as the passions and bring him to you. Do not be worried," said they; and drawing near the Blessed One they said to him, "O monk, we will attend on you as your wives." The Blessed One neither paid any attention to what they said nor opened his eyes to look at them. As his mind had reached the state of perfect emancipation on the destruction of all material substrata, he sat there experiencing the bliss of absolute

---

[1] "Desire, Aversion, and Lust".

calm. Then again the daughters of Māra went up to the Blessed One six times, saying, "O monk, we will attend on you as your wives," each one having miraculously presented herself in a hundred different guises as virgins, as women who had not borne children, who had given birth to one child, or who had had two children, or as women in middle age, or as elderly women, thinking to themselves, "Varied are the expectations of men; some are attracted by virgins, some by women in the prime of youth, some by women in middle age, and some others by older women. Let us then entice him in all possible ways." And the Blessed One paid no attention even to that, for he had gained perfect emancipation on the destruction of all material substrata.

But some teachers say that when the Blessed One saw them approaching him disguised as elderly women he resolved that they should continue to remain like that forever, with their broken teeth and grey hair. This should not be accepted, for the Teacher would not make such a resolution. But the Blessed One said, "Go away from here. To what purpose do you strive thus? It is not proper that you should act thus even in the presence of those who have not overcome their lust. As for the Tathāgata, he has overcome lust, ill-will, and delusion." And he preached to them a discourse with the following two verses dealing with his destruction of defilements, which occur in the Buddhavagga of the Dhammapada:[1]

280. He whose conquest cannot be wrested away from him, and none in the world[2] pursues the conquest he has made, by what path can you lead him, the Enlightened One, of limitless ken, the path-free?

281. He to whom there exists no ensnaring worldly attachment to craving to lead him astray anywhere, by what path can you lead him, the Enlightened One, of limitless ken, the path-free?

Mucalinda

They returned to their father telling each other, "Truly has our father spoken; the Sugata is the Worthy One in the world, [**80**] for he cannot easily be led away by worldly desire." And the Blessed One

---

[1]Dhp 179–80.

[2]I.e. the Defilements.

spent seven days there and repaired to the Mucalinda tree. There he spent a week in perfect security, experiencing the bliss of emancipation as though inside his scented bedchamber, seated within the folds of the *nāga* king Mucalinda[1] who had wound his coils round him seven times to ward off the cold and other inclemencies when rainy weather continued for a whole week. From there he went to the Rājāyatana[2] tree. There too he sat experiencing the bliss of emancipation. With this he completed seven weeks. During this interval he did not [feel the need to] wash his face, attend to bodily ablutions, and eat any food. He spent the time in the bliss of the ecstacy of [*jhāna*-] meditation, of the Path, and of the Fruits.

Then on the forty-ninth day, when the seven weeks were over, as he sat there he felt the need to wash his face. Sakka, the king of the deities, brought with him a medicinal myrobalan [gallnut] fruit. The Teacher ate it and with it his bowels were cleansed. Sakka next brought him a toothstick of Nāgalatā wood and water for washing his face. And the Teacher used that toothstick, and washed his face with that water which was brought from the lake Anotatta, and again sat down there at the foot of the Rājāyatana tree.

Tapassu and Bhalluka

At this time two merchants known as Tapassu and Bhalluka, who were travelling from the district of Ukkala to the Middle Country with a caravan of five hundred carts, were incited by a deity, a former blood-relation of theirs; and they stopped their carts to make a gift of food to the Teacher. They went to the Teacher taking with them a rice cake and a honey comb; they implored him, "O Lord, may the Blessed One accept this food from us with compassion towards us," and stood beside him. Since his bowl had disappeared on the very day he accepted [Sujātā's] milk rice, he began to wonder how he should accept it, for Tathāgatas do not receive food in their hands. Thereupon the four Guardian Deities who knew what he was thinking about came from the four directions bringing four bowls made of sapphire, and offered them to him. The Blessed One refused to accept them. They next brought him

[1]Named after the *Mucalinda* tree, *Barringtonia acutangula*, Sinhalese *midella*.

[2]*Buchania latifolia* (*PED*).

four bowls made of granite.[6] Out of consideration for the four deities the Blessed One accepted all the four bowls and, placing one on top of the other, resolved that they should become one. And these four became one bowl of medium size with distinct lines appearing at the mouth. The Blessed One accepted the food in that newly made bowl of granite and offered thanks. The two brothers who were merchants took refuge in the Buddha and the Dhamma [**81**] and became lay disciples uttering the twofold formula. Then to them, who requested him, "Lord, give us something that we may continually honour," he gave a few hair relics from his head having plucked them out stroking his head with his right hand. Enshrining these relics they built a monument in their city.

Brahmā's Solicitation

As for the Perfectly Enlightened One, he rose from there and made his way again to the Ajapāla Banyan tree and sat down at its foot. And the moment he sat there, as he was reflecting on the profundity of the Dhamma he had realised, there arose in him the thought customary with all Buddhas, that he had realised the Dhamma but that he was not inclined to proclaim the Dhamma to others. Thereupon Brahmā Sahampati, exclaiming "Alas, the world is in peril! Alas, the world faces grave disaster!", went before the Teacher rallying the Sakkas, Suyāmas, Santusitas, Sunimmita-vasavattis, and the Great Brahmās and implored him to proclaim the Teaching with such requests as, "Lord, may the Blessed One preach the Dhamma, may the Sugata preach the Dhamma."

His Journey to Bārāṇasī

The Teacher gave him the assurance, and thinking to himself, "To whom am I to proclaim the Dhamma first?", he concluded, "Āḷāra is wise, he will soon comprehend it"; but surveying again with his divine eye he perceived that he had died a week prior to then and directed his thoughts on Uddaka. Realizing that he too had died the previous evening he thought of the Pañcavaggiyas, saying to himself, "The monks of the Group of Five have been of great service to me." Reflecting, "Where would they be dwelling now?", he perceived that it was in the Deer Park at Bārāṇasī and made up his mind, "I will go there

---

[6] Lit. "stone of the colour of a green pea".

and set rolling the Wheel of the Dhamma." He spent a few days begging his alms in the neighbourhood of the Bodhi tree, and thinking of going to Bārāṇasi on the full-moon day of Āsāḷhi he entered the highroad eighteen *yojanas* long, taking his bowl and robe early in the morning at daybreak on the fourteenth day of the fortnight. On the way he met the wandering ascetic Upaka and announced to him his attainment of Enlightenment, and on the same day he reached Isipatana in the evening.

The Pañcavaggiyas

The Elders of the Group of Five, seeing from afar the Tathāgata coming in their direction, made an agreement among themselves, "Friends, here comes the mendicant Gotama with body well nourished, faculties made active, and with body golden in colour as a result of his reversion to a life of luxury. We will not rise to receive him. Since he should be honoured with a seat as he is born of noble family we will merely prepare a seat for him." The Blessed One, with his insight which has the power to reveal to him the thoughts that pass in the minds of beings of this world including the deities, reflected on what they were thinking and knew their thoughts. [**82**] Then, concentrating his thoughts of loving kindness which pervade all deities and men with no restriction, he directed them specifically on them. They were pervaded by the thoughts of loving kindness of the Blessed One, and were unable to abide by their decision as the Tathāgata gradually drew near them; and [so] they discharged all their obligations [to a guest] such as greeting him, rising to receive him and so forth. And as they were ignorant of his attainment of Enlightenment they continued to address him either by name or with the appellation "Friend".

The Proclamation of the Wheel of the Dhamma

Then the Blessed One announced to them his attainment of Enlightenment saying, "Brethren, do not address the Tathāgata by his name or with the appellation, 'Friend'; for, O Brethren, the Tathāgata is the Worthy One, he is perfectly Enlightened." Seated in the seat prepared as became a Buddha and surrounded by eighteen crores of Brahmās, he addressed the Pañcavaggiya Elders and preached to them the Discourse of the Proclamation of the Wheel of the Dhamma,[1] while

[1]Dhammacakkapavattana Sutta, Vin I 10–12, S V 420–23.

the lunar mansion of Āsāḷha was on its descendant. Among these five, the Elder Aññākondañña, who began to direct his wisdom in accordance with the discourse, along with the eighteen crores of Brahmās, established himself in the Fruit of the Stream-Entrant stage at the conclusion of the Sutta. The Teacher, who took up his residence there for the rainy season, remained seated in the dwelling there on the following day giving instruction to the Elder Vappa. The other four went begging for alms. The Elder Vappa gained the Fruit of the Stream-Entrant stage in that very forenoon. In the selfsame manner he established all of them in the Fruit of the Stream-Entrant stage, the Elder Bhaddiya the next day, the Elder Mahānāma the next day, and the Elder Assaji the next day, and on the fifth day of the lunar fortnight he summoned all five of them and preached to them the Discourse on the Characteristics of Egolessness.[1] At the conclusion of the discourse all the five Elders were established in the Fruit of Arahantship.

The Clansman Yasa

Subsequently the Teacher, who saw the clansman Yasa's good fortune to [be able to] attain the Paths, summoned him with the words, "Come, Yasa!" as he was going away at night, leaving his house behind with revulsion for it. He established him in the Stream-Entrant stage that very night and in Arahantship on the following day, and also gave ordination to his fifty-four compansions with the formula, "Come, monks!", and established them in Arahantship as well.

The Bhaddavaggiyas

In this manner when there were sixty-one Arahants in the world, the Teacher, having spent the Rains' Retreat, performed the "Invitation" ceremony at its conclusion and sent the sixty monks in sixty different directions exhorting them with the words, "Wander forth, monks, on tours of service"; going himself on his way to Uruvelā he met the thirty Bhaddavaggiya (Members of the Happy Band) Princes in the Kappāsiya forest on the way thither and disciplined them in the Paths. The least advanced of them became a Stream-Entrant while the most progressive among them became a Non-Returner.

[1] Anattalakkhaṇa Sutta, Vin I 13–14, S III 66–68.

The Three Brothers, Matted-hair Ascetics

He ordained all of them with the formula, "Come, monks!", and sending them in different directions he himself repaired to Uruvelā and disciplined in the Paths the three brothers, the matted-hair ascetics Uruvela Kassapa and others, together with their following of a thousand matted-hair ascetics, by showing them three and a half thousand miracles; giving them the ordination with the formula, "Come, monks!", he seated them at Gayāsīsa and established them in Arahatship with the Discourse on the Parable of Fire,[1] and attended by those thousand Arahants [**83**] he went to the pleasure grove of Laṭṭhivana on the outskirts of the city of Rājagaha with the intention of redeeming the promise made to King Bimbisāra.

King Bimbisāra

The king, having heard from the keeper of the park that the Teacher had come, went to see the Teacher attended by a retinue of twelve *nahutas* of brahmans and householders; and falling prostrate at the feet of the Tathāgata, whose soles bore the emblems of the wheels radiating a lustre resembling a circular canopy of gold, sat on one side together with his retinue. Thereupon the following thought occurred to those brahmans and householders, "What then? Does the Great Recluse practise the higher life under Uruvela Kassapa or does Uruvela Kassapa practise it under the Great Recluse?" The Blessed One understood in his mind the reflection that was passing in their minds and addressed the Elder [Kassapa] in a stanza:

282 Seeing what advantage, O inhabitant of Uruvelā, have you forsaken your fire sacrifice? For you claim to practise austere vows [which lead to emanciation]. I ask you Kassapa this question: How is it that your fire sacrifice has been given up?

And the Elder, who knew what the Blessed One's intention was, replied:

283. Sacrifices speak of [pleasant] forms, sounds and also tastes as well as other enjoyments and women. As I have realised that this is a

[1] Ādittapariyāya Sutta, Vin I 34–35, S IV 19–20.

taint in the sphere of the material substrata I have therefore found no delight in sacrifices and oblations.

Having uttered this stanza, in order to disclose to the others that he was the disciple he placed his head on the footstool of the Tathāgata, saying, "Lord, the Blessed One is my Teacher and I am the disciple"; and he rose into the air seven times as far as the height of seven palm trees, beginning with that of one palm tree, two, three, and so on, and descending again saluted the Tathāgata and sat respectfully beside him. Seeing that wonder the populace began to speak in praise of the virtues of the Teacher, saying, "Ah, how great is the power of the Buddha! Even Uruvela Kassapa, whose dogmatic beliefs were so strong, considers him worthy and has broken asunder his net of heresy, being disciplined by the Tathagata!" The Blessed One, saying, "It is not only now that I have conquered Uruvela Kassapa, but also in the past has he been disciplined by me," narrated the Mahānāradakassapa Jātaka (No. 544) in connection with this incident, and declared the Four Noble Truths. The King of Magadha became established in the Fruit of the Stream-Entrant stage together with eleven *nahutas* of his followers. And one *nahuta* proclaimed themselves lay disciples. [**84**]

The king, seated there as he was near the Teacher, conveyed to him his five wishes,[1] sought the Refuges, invited him for the morrow's meal, and rose from his seat and departed going round the Blessed One reverentially. On the following day, all the citizens of Rājagaha, eighteen crores in number, both those who had seen the Blessed One and those who had not, left Rājagaha early in the morning and went to Laṭṭhivana wishing to pay their respects to the Tathāgata. The road, three *gāvutas* long, could not contain them all. The entire Laṭṭhivana grove was crowded all the time. And the multitude beholding the most handsome physical form of the Blessed One could not restrain their delight. This is called the Vaṇṇabhūmi (the field of praise). On occasions such as these all the splendour of the physical frame of a Tathāgata in the diverse aspects of the major and minor characteristics must necessarily be praised.

---

[1]See Vin I 37.

Sakka

There was no room for even a single monk to leave when the park and the road were all the time crowded with the multitude, who were thus gazing upon the exceeding splendour of the form of the Lord of Ten Powers. And on that day the seat on which Sakka was seated turned hot [to indicate to him] that the Blessed One might miss his meal and that this should not happen. On circumspection he became aware of that fact, and assuming the form of a young brahman descended in front of the Buddha; making way for him by his divine power he walked in front of the Teacher, singing his praises in the following panegyrics, extolling the virtues of the Buddha, Dhamma, and the Saṅgha:

284. The self-controlled one with the self-controlled and erstwhile matted-hair ascetics who are released at heart, the Blessed One with his body radiant as burnished gold has entered Rājagaha.
285. The emancipated one, with the emancipated and erstwhile matted-hair ascetics who are emancipated at heart, the Blessed One with his body radiant as burnished gold has entered Rājagaha.
286. He who has crossed over [the Flood], with them who had crossed over, the erstwhile matted-hair ascetics who are emancipated at heart, the Blessed One with his body radiant as burnished gold has entered Rājagaha.
287. He who is possessed of the ten Noble States[1] and of the Ten Powers, the knower of the Ten Phenomena,[2] endowed with the ten attributes, the Blessed One has entered Rājagaha with a following of ten hundred.

The multitude, beholding the handsome figure of the youth, thought, "This young man is exceedingly handsome, but we have not seen him before"; and asked, "From where does this youth come, and whose son is he?" Hearing this the brahman youth replied with the stanza:

---

[1]*Dasa ariyavāsa*, see D III 269, 291.

[2]*Dasadhammavidū*, cp. Vin I 38, where the commentary (Sp 973) glosses as the ten "paths of *kamma*" (*kammapathā*, see *PED* s.v.).

288. He who is wise, restrained in all spheres, awakened, the unrivalled, the worthy, the well-farer in this world — his attendant am I.

The Acceptance of Veḷuvana

The Teacher entered upon the path that was cleared by Sakka [**85**] and entered Rājagaha attended by a retinue of a thousand monks. The king gave sumptuous alms to the Brotherhood with the Buddha at their head, and taking into his hands water scented with the perfumes of flowers together with the golden water pot in which it was, he poured the water over the hand of the Lord of Ten Powers dedicating the Bamboo Grove (Veḷuvana), with the words, "Lord, I cannot live without the Three Gems. I wish to visit the Blessed One at all times whether it is the time to visit or not. But the Laṭṭhivana is situated too far, whereas our royal park Veḷuvana lies close at hand, it is easy of access and a worthy residence for the Buddha. May the Blessed One accept it from me!" On the occasion of the acceptance of that park the great earth shook commemorating the firm establishment of the roots of the Dispensation of the Buddha. In all Jambudīpa there is no other dwelling place save Veḷuvana whose acceptance was accompanied by an earthquake; and in the Island of Tambapaṇṇi (Sri Lanka), none other than the Great Monastery at whose acceptance the earth shook. The Teacher accepted the dwelling place at the Bamboo Grove, preached to the king a discourse gladdening him, rose from his, and went to the Bamboo Grove attended by his retinue of monks.

Sāriputta and Moggallāna

And at this time two wandering ascetics named Sāriputta and Moggallāna were living at Rājagaha begging their food there, seeking after immortality. Sāriputta had seen the Elder Assaji on his begging round, and waited on him with devotion at heart; hearing from him the stanza beginning with, "Those phenomena which proceed from causes", he attained the Fruit of the Stream-Entrant stage, and repeated the same stanza to his companion the mendicant Moggallāna. He too was established in the Fruit of the Stream-Entrant stage. Both of them, with the approval of [their teacher] Sañjaya went away with their followers and received ordination under the Teacher. Of the two, Mahāmoggallāna became an Arahant within a week and the Elder Sāriputta within a fortnight. And the Teacher appointed the two of them his chief disciples. On the very day the Elder Sāriputta attained Arahantship an assembly of disciples was summoned.

King Suddhodana Wishes to See His Son

Whilst the Tathāgata was living there in the Veḷuvana park, the great king Suddhodana heard that his son, who had engaged himself in the practice of severe austerities, had attained to Perfect Enlightenment and had set rolling the wheel of the Dhamma, was residing in the Bamboo Grove depending on Rājagaha for alms; and he said to one of the ministers, "Come, friend, go to Rājagaha with a retinue of a thousand men and command him in my name, 'Your father, King Suddhodana wishes to see you,' and come hither bringing my son along." Saying, "Very well, Your Majesty," he accepted the king's command with head bent low, and before long he went the distance of sixty *yojanas* in the company of his thousand followers; they entered the monastery at the time the Lord of Ten Powers was preaching the Dhamma seated amidst the fourfold assembly. Thinking, "Let the king's message wait a while," he listened to the Teacher's discourse standing at the back of the assembly; [**86**] and attaining Arahatship together with those thousand men, he begged for ordination. The Blessed One stretched forth his right hand saying, "Come, monks," and immediately, all of them stood there, with robes and bowls miraculously obtained, like Elders of a hundred years' religious experience. From the time they attained Arahatship they refrained from delivering the king's message to the Lord of Ten Powers, thinking that it would interfere with their impartiality, which is characteristic of the Worthy Ones. As for the king, he sent another minister in the same manner as before, telling him, "Come, friend, you go: he who has gone before has not returned nor has the message been delivered." He too went, and in the same manner as the first gained Arahantship together with his followers, and remained silent. In the same manner the king sent nine other ministers with retinues of a thousand followers each. And all them having accomplished their aim remained there observing silence.

Kāḷudāyī

The king, who was not able to find one who would bring even a message to him, thought to himself, "So many have I sent and not one among them has brought a message back to me through their lack of loyalty." And examining among all his courtiers "Who will now carry out my request?", he thought of Kāḷudāyī. It is said that he was the minister who carried out every wish of the king, was acquainted with all the internal affairs and most trustworthy, born on the same day the Bodhisatta was born, his companion and playfellow in childhood. The king summoned him and said to him, "Dear Kāḷudāyī, in my eagerness to see my son I have sent to him nine thousand men, but not one have I found who would come back even with mere tidings of him. And it is uncertain whether any danger might befall my life; it is my anxious wish that I should see my son before I die. Will you be able to bring my son to me so that I may see him?"

"Your Majesty, I will be able to accomplish it, if I am allowed to join the Order."

"Dear friend, join the Order or not as you wish, but bring my son to me so that I may see him."

"Very well, Your Majesty," said he, and taking the king's message he went to Rājagaha, and standing at the back of the assembly at the time the Teacher was preaching the doctrine he listened to the Dhamma, gained the Fruits of Arahantship together with his followers, and received ordination with the formula, "Come, monks". The Teacher, after his attainment of Enlightenment spent the first rainy season at Isipatana. After spending the Retreat and having performed the "Invitation" ceremony he went to Uruvelā; living there for three months he disciplined the three brothers, the matted-hair ascetics, and returned to Rājagaha on the full-moon day of the month of Phussa, with a following of a thousand monks, and lived there for two months. Up to this time five months had elapsed from the day he set out from Bārāṇasi. The whole of the winter season was past. And seven or eight days had elapsed from the day of the arrival of the Elder Udāyī. On the full-moon day of Phagguṇa, Udāyī thought, "The winter is over, the spring has set in; men have gathered their harvest and left it on the roads for removal at convenient places, the earth is covered with lush green grass, the woods are in full flowering, the roads are suitable for travel, and it is time for the Lord of Ten Powers to honour his kinsmen with a visit." And going up to the Blessed One he sang, in about sixty stanzas, praise of the journey in order to induce the Lord of Ten Powers to visit his native town, thus:[1] [**87**]

289. The trees, dear Lord, are now like glowing embers: they have cast off their foliage being in quest of fruit; they shine like fire with flames, and, O Great Hero, the season is full of delights.

290. It is neither too cold, nor is it too warm; there is no famine in the land; the earth is covered with fresh green pasture; this O Great Sage, is the time to set out.

The Blessed One Visits Kapilavatthu

Then the Teacher asked him, "Udāyī, why is it that you sing the joys of travel in so sweet a voice?"

"Lord, your father King Suddhodana wishes to see you; do honour to your kinsmen with a visit."

"Very well, Udāyī, I will show favour to my kinsmen. Tell the Brotherhood of monks that they shall fulfil the duties connected with journeying from place to place."

"Yes, Lord," said the Elder and informed them of it. The Blessed One set out from Rājagaha, attended in all by twenty thousand monks freed from their banes, ten thousand clansmen from Aṅga and Magadha and ten thousand from Kapilavatthu, and travelled a *yojana* in a day. He continued on a leisurely sojourn with the intention of reaching Kapilavatthu which was sixty *yojanas* from Rājagaha, in two months.

Kāḷudāyī Receives Alms at Kapilavatthu

Thinking that he would inform the king that the Blessed One had set out, the Elder rose into the sky and appeared at the king's palace. The king was delighted at the arrival of the Elder and made him sit down on a magnificent couch; filling a bowl with the most delicious food prepared for himself, he gave it to him. The Elder rose from his seat and indicated that he was ready to depart.

---

[1]See Th 527 foll., which gives ten verses including the two given here.

"Sit down and eat," said the king.

"Your Majesty, I will go back to my Teacher and eat the food."

"Where then, is the Teacher?"

"Your Majesty, he has already set out on his journey in the company of twenty thousand monks, to see you."

The king was pleased to hear it and said, "You partake of this food; and until my son arrives at this city you take food to him from here." The Elder consented.

The king waited on the Elder, had the bowl cleaned with perfumed powder, and filling it with the best food placed it in the Elder's hand saying, "Take this to the Tathāgata." The Elder, while everyone was looking on, threw the bowl into the sky and himself rose into the air and taking the food to the Teacher placed it in his hand. The Teacher partook of it. In this manner, the Elder brought food every day. And the Teacher thus ate the food provided by the king all along the journey. The Elder too, when he had finished his meal every day, [**88**] won over the minds of all the members of the royal household in favour of the Teacher even before they had seen him, by talking to them of the virtues of the Buddha and telling them, "Today the Blessed One has come so far and so far today." Therefore has the Blessed One assigned to him the highest place in this respect, saying, "He indeed is the highest among those of my disciples who can arouse the faith of families, namely Kāḷudāyī."[1]

The Blessed One Performs a Miracle

And the Sākiyas too discussed among themselves in assembly, "When the Blessed One arrives here we shall be able to see our most distinguished kinsman", and concerned themselves over a place of residence for the Blessed One. They decided that the Park of the Sākyan Nigrodha was a suitable place, and making all arrangements to suit his convenience they went forward to receive him carrying perfumes and flowers in their hands, having sent ahead of them young boys and girls

[1] A I 25.

of the city decked in all their finery. Then followed the princes and princesses of the noble families. Next to them, they themselves conducted the Blessed One to the Nigrodha Grove honouring him with perfumes, flowers, powders, and the like. There the Blessed One sat down on the seat specially prepared for the Buddha, surrounded by the twenty thousand canker-free Arahants. The Sākiyas are proud by nature and stubborn in their arrogance. Thinking, "Prince Siddhattha is younger than us, he is in relationship our younger brother, our nephew, our son, our grandson, and so on," they told the younger members of the noble families, "You pay homage to him, we will sit behind you." When they were thus seated the Blessed One perceived his kinsmen's intention not to pay homage to him, and in order to make them do reverence to him he entered the ecstasy (*jhāna*) which is the basis of intuitive knowledge, and emerging from it he rose into the air as if scattering the dust on his feet upon their heads and performed a miracle which resembled the miracle of the double performed at the foot of the Gaṇḍamba tree.

The Sākiyas Pay Homage to the Blessed One

The king saw that miracle and said, "O Blessed One, I worshipped you when I saw your feet turning round and planting themselves on the Brahman's head on the day of your birth when I brought you out to pay homage to Kāḷadevala. This was my first obeisance. I paid homage at your feet when I saw that the shadow did not turn while you were seated on the royal couch under the shade of the rose-apple tree on the day of the ploughing festival. That was my second obeisance. Now also, seeing this miracle, the like of which I had not seen before, I pay homage to your feet. This is my third obeisance." When the king had paid him homage, there was not a single Sākiya who was able to remain there without making obeisance to the Blessed One. All of them paid him homage. In this manner the Blessed One made his relatives pay homage to him, and descending from the sky sat down on the seat prepared for him. When the Blessed One was seated the assembly of kinsmen had swelled to its highest capacity. All of them sat down with their minds intent. Thereupon a large rain-cloud poured forth a lotus-shower (*pokkhara-vassa*). Streams of copper-coloured water flowed beneath making a rumbling noise. Those who wished to get wet got wet, but not even a drop fell on those who did not wish to get wet. Seeing this, every one was awed and wonder-struck and exclaimed, "Ah, a miracle! Ah, a great miracle!" The Teacher said [**89**], "It is not only now that a lotus-shower came down by my power whilst seated in the assembly of my kinsmen, but also in the past", and narrated the Birth Story of Vessantara (Jātaka No. 547) in connection with this incident. When they had finished listening to the discourse all of them rose from their seats, saluted him, and departed. But there was not one among them, whether king or minister of state, who said, "Accept a meal from us tomorrow," before he went away.

The Blessed One Begs Alms in the City

On the following day, the Teacher, attended by twenty thousand monks, entered the streets of Kapilavatthu to beg alms. No one came to him and invited him for a meal or took his bowl. Standing beside the stake driven in at the city gate the Blessed One reflected, "How did former Buddhas go, begging their food in their native cities? Did they first of all go, not in due order, to the houses of the nobility? Or did they beg from door to door in due order?" Seeing that not one Buddha had gone to the houses that were not in due order, he began his alms round from door to door, beginning from the house situated at the [outer] end, saying to himself, "I too must accept as mine this tradition, this legacy, so that in the future my disciples pursuing their training under me will fulfil the duties connected with the begging of their daily food."

Hearing that their master Prince Siddhattha was going about begging his food, the people threw open the attic windows in two-storeyed and three-storeyed houses and gazed on with curiosity. The queen, mother of Rāhula herself, said, "My lord and master who was acccustomed to going about in this city in gilded palanquins and other conveyances, in all regal splendour, now goes about begging his food carrying [an earthenware] bowl with shaven hair and beard and clad in yellow robes; does this become him?" Opening her attic window and looking out she saw the Blessed One radiant in the unparalleled majesty of a Buddha all over his person from his topknot right down to his feet, adorned with the thirty-two distinct marks of a Great Being, shining with the eighty minor marks, all encompassed within the fathom-deep halo that spread right round him, and illuminating the city streets with his bodily radiance which spread in clusters of many colours.

And she sang his praises with the eight Narasīha Gāthā (the Stanzas on the Lion among Men), which began with,

291. His hair is glossy, dark, soft, and curly; his broad forehead is spotless as the sun; his long nose is well-proportioned, raised upward and delicate; the lion among men is covered with a mass of rays;

and announced to the king, "Your son is going about begging his food." The king was deeply agitated on hearing this and left the place in great haste, gathering up the folds of his robe in his hand; he ran and stood in front of the Blessed One, saying, "Lord, why do you bring disgrace upon us? Why do you go about begging your food? Why do you give the impression [to others] that it is not possible to feed so many monks?" **[90]**

"Your Majesty, this is the customary practice of our lineage."

"Lord, is not the Khattiya descent from Mahāsammata our lineage? And in this lineage there was not one Khattiya who went about begging alms."

"Your Majesty, this royal lineage is your descent, but mine is this lineage of Buddhas, from Dīpaṅkara, Kondañña, and others right down to Kassapa. These, and many other Buddhas, thousands in number, have begged their daily food and lived on the alms gathered by them." Standing as he was in the middle of the street he uttered the verse:

292. Rise up and be not indolent,[1] lead a life of righteousness. He who leads a righteous life remains in bliss both in this world and in the next.

At the end of the recitation of the verse the king attained the Fruit of the Stream-Entrant stage.

293. Lead a life of righteousness, and do not practise misdeeds. He who leads a righgeous life remains in bliss both in this world and in the next.

---

[1]This phrase is traditionally interpreted as "be not heedless in the gathering of alms food" (*ud-śiṣ-ṭa* > *ucchiṭṭha/uttiṭṭha*).

And having listened to the above verse he attained the Fruit of the Once-Returner stage. When he heard the Birth Story of Mahādhammapāla (Jātaka No. 447) he attained the Fruit of the Non-Returner stage. He attained Arahatship at the time of his death as he lay on his royal couch under the white canopy of state. No necessity arose for the king to engage in striving, leading a life of seclusion in the forest. It was only when he had realized the Fruit of the Stream-Entrant stage that he took the bowl of the Blessed One, and conducted him together with his retinue to the royal palace and served them with delicious food, both hard and soft. And when he had partaken of his meal, all the women of the royal household, excepting the mother of Rāhula, came and paid homage to the Blessed One. But she, even though she was told by her attendants, "Go Lady, and pay homage to our master," did not go, saying, "If there is any virtue in me, my lord will come to me himself; when he comes to me I will worship him."

Rāhula's Mother Pays Homage

The Blessed One, with the king carrying the bowl for him, entered the royal apartments of the princess, together with his two chief disciples. He told them that nothing should be said to her when the princess worshipped him in [whatever] manner she desired, and sat down on the seat prepared for him. She hastened there, and holding him by his ankles, rolled her head on his feet worshipping him as she had desired. The king spoke of her virtues, such as the esteem and regard the princess bore for the Blessed One: "Lord, when my daughter[-in-law] heard that you were wearing yellow robes, **[91]** from that day she herself began to wear yellow garments. When she heard that you were taking only one meal a day, she too began to take only one meal a day. When she heard that you had given up the use of comfortable couches, she began to sleep on a bed of planks. When she heard that you had given up the use of garlands, perfumes, and so forth, she too gave up using them. When her relatives sent a message, saying, 'We will look after you', she did not look to any one of them. O Blessed One, my daughter possesses such virtues."

"This is not a wonder, your majesty, that the princess should take care of herself when her wisdom is mature, having you also as her guardian. In the past, wandering alone among the mountains with no one to protect her, while yet her wisdom was not mature, she looked after herself." Saying so he narrated the Birth Story of the Candakinnara (Jātaka No. 485) and rising from his seat, departed.

Nanda

On the following day, when the ceremonies of the consecration, housewarming, and marriage of Prince Nanda were being celebrated, he went to his house, and wishing to ordain him, made the prince carry the bowl; giving his blessings, he rose from his seat and went away. And Janapadakalyāṇī,[1] seeing the prince depart, craned her neck and looked at him and said, "Come back soon, my Lord." Nanda did not have the courage to ask the Blessed One to take his bowl, and went [all the way] to the monastery. Even without his wish the Blessed One gave him the ordination. In this manner, on the third day after his arrival in the City of Kapila, the Blessed One ordained Nanda.

Rāhula

On the seventh day, the mother of Rāhula dressed the prince in his best attire and sent him to the Blessed One, saying, "Look, child, at this monk with a golden complexion, glorious as a manifestation of Brahmā and attended by twenty thousand monks! He is your father. He owned many great treasures, but from the time he renounced home we have not seen them. Go to him and ask him for your inheritance, saying, 'Dear father, I am your son; after my consecration I wish to become a Universal Ruler. I need wealth. Give me your treasures, for a son is heir to his father's possessions.'" The boy went to the Blessed One, and with his affection kindled towards his father he stood there highly delighted, saying, "O monk, even your shadow is pleasant," and making many such statements which were to be expected of him.

Rāhula's Ordination

Meanwhile, the Blessed One, who had finished his meal, made the donors participate in the merit and set out rising from his seat. The prince followed the Blessed One, saying, "O monk, give me my inheritance. Give me my inheritance, O monk!" The Blessed One did

---

[1] "The prettiest maiden of the district", the bride.

not turn the child back. Even the attendants were not able to prevent him following the Blessed One. In this manner he accompanied the Blessed One right up to the monastery. Then the Blessed One reflected, "This wealth that belongs to his father which he asks for leads to Saṃsāra, and is bound up with suffering; therefore let me give him the sevenfold noble treasure which I received at the foot of the Bodhi tree, and I will make him the heir to the transcendental inheritance." He addressed Sāriputta, [**92**] "Now, Sāriputta, ordain Prince Rāhula."

The King's Attainment of the Fruits of the Non-Returner Stage

When the prince had been ordained intense grief arose in the king. Not being able to endure it any longer he told the Blessed One, and requested a boon from him: "Lord, it would be well if the venerable ones do not ordain a child who has not received his parents' consent!" The Blessed One granted him the boon, and on the following day, after he had had his morning meal at the king's palace, the king who was seated aside told him, "Lord, during your practice of severe austerities a deity came to me and told me that my son was dead; I refused to believe what he said and told him that my son would not die before his attainment of Enlightenment." He replied, "How will you believe him now, when in the past you were shown bones and told that your son was dead and you did not believe those words?", and narrated the Birth Story of Mahādhammapāla (Jātaka No. 447) in connection with it. At the end of the discourse the king attained the Fruit of the Non-Returner stage.

Anāthapiṇḍika

In this manner the Blessed One established his father in the three Fruits, and returned to Rājagaha to take up his residence at Sītavana. At this time the householder Anāthapiṇḍika visited the house of his intimate friend, the merchant prince of Rājagaha, carrying five hundred wagonloads of merchandise. He heard that the Buddha had appeared in the world, and at early dawn visited the Teacher by the gate that was opened for him by the supernatural power of the deities. He listened to the doctrine and gained the Fruit of the Stream-Entrant stage. On the following day he gave sumptuous alms to the Brotherhood of monks with the Buddha at their head, and making the Teacher promise that he would visit Sāvatthi, erected monasteries all along the route of forty-five *yojanas* leading there, spending for each one of them a hundred thousand pieces, and bought Jeta's Grove for eighteen thousand crores of gold pieces laying them from end to end [to cover the surface of the park] and renovated the place. In the centre he erected the Fragrant Bed-chamber for the Buddha; and around it, on that pleasant site, at the expense of a further eighteen crores of gold pieces, he caused the building of a delightful monastery complete with separate dwellings for the eighty great Elders, other lodgings consisting of single-walled and double-walled buildings, long halls decorated with rows of geese and quails, pavilions, ponds, cloisters, and places for meditation at daytime and at night; and he sent a message inviting the Lord of Ten Powers. On hearing the words of the messenger, the Teacher set out from Rājagaha with a large retinue of monks and reached the city of Sāvatthi in due course.

The Acceptance of Jetavana

Then the great merchant prince arranged the ceremony of the dedication of the monastery, and on the day of the arrival of the Tathāgata at Jetavana, sent his son decked with all ornaments together with five hundred other boys also in festive attire. He, together with his retinue carrying five hundred banners radiant with cloth of five different colours, went ahead of the Blessed One. [**93**] Behind them followed Mahāsubhaddā and Cūlasubhaddā, the two daughters of the merchant prince, together with the five hundred maidens carrying water pots filled to the brim. Behind them walked the merchant prince's wife decked in all her spendour, attended by five hundred women carrying filled bowls. Behind all of them came the great merchant prince himself, dressed in new garments, accompanied by five hundred other merchant princes also dressed in new garments, and he went forward to meet the Blessed One.

Sending this band of lay disciples ahead of him, the Blessed One, attended by his large retinue of monks, entered the monastery of Jetavana with his unequalled glory and infinte grace of a Buddha, as though with the radiance from his body turning the forest groves into clusters of feathers sprayed with the essence of gold. Thereupon Anāthapiṇḍika asked him, "Lord, how shall I act in connection with this monastery?"

"Now, O householder, dedicate this monastery to the Brotherhood of monks whether present here or to come hither hereafter."

"Yes, my Lord," said the great merchant prince; and taking a golden water pot he poured the water of dedication on the hand of the Lord of Ten Powers and offered it saying, "I give this monastery of Jetavana to the Brotherhood of monks with the Buddha at their head, to those of the four quarters whether present or to come hither hereafter."

In Praise of the Dedication of Monasteries

The Teacher accepted the monastery and spoke of the advantages of donating monasteries in his sermon, making them participate in the merit:

294. They ward off cold and heat, also wild beasts, serpents, and insects and rain in the winter.
295. When high winds and intense heat arise, it wards them off. The gift of a dwelling to the Brotherhood of monks as a place of safety and comfort, to meditate and to gain insight, is extolled by the Buddha as the highest gift.
296. Therefore let a wise man who foresees his own welfare build delightful monasteries and house learned monks in them.
297. And with delighted mind let him give food and drink, clothes and lodgings to the upright among them. [**94**]
298. They preach to him the doctrine which delivers him from all pain; and realizing this Dhamma here, he obtains perfect release, being freed from the banes.

From the following day, Anāthapiṇḍika commenced the festival of the dedication of the monastery. The festival of the dedication of Visākhā's mansion was over in four months, but Anāthapiṇḍika's festival of dedication took nine months to finish. And even for this ceremony the expenses came to eighteen crores. Thus for this monastery alone, he spent fifty-four crores.

Jetavana as the Residence of all Buddhas

In the past, during the time of the Blessed One Vipassī, the merchant prince named Punabbasumitta bought this land by spreading golden bricks over it, and erected on the identical spot a monastery extending a *yojana*. In the time of the Blessed One Vessabhū, a merchant prince named Sotthiya bought this land by placing over it elephant feet made of gold, and built on the identical spot a monastery extending half a *yojana*. In the time of the Blessed One Kakusandha a merchant prince named Accuta bought this land by placing golden bricks over it and built on the identical spot a monastery extending one *gāvuta*. In the time of the Blessed One Koṇāgamana a merchant prince named Ugga bought this land by laying golden turtles over it, and built on the identical spot a monastery extending half a *gāvuta*. In the time of the Blessed One Kassapa, a merchant prince named Sumaṅgala bought this land by laying golden bricks over it, and built on the identical spot a monastery sixteen *karīsas*[1] in extent. And in the time of our Blessed One, the merchant prince Anāthapiṇḍika bought this land by laying a crore of *kahāpaṇa*s, and built on the same spot a monastery extending eight *karīsas*. Thus, this spot has not been deserted by any of the Buddhas.

In this manner, wherever the Blessed One lived, from the time of his attainment of Enlightenment at the foot of the great Bodhi tree up to his deathbed at the Great Parinibbāna, is included in the Recent Epoch. And now we will expound all the Birth Stories in relation to it.

The End of the Introductory Episode of the Commentary to the Birth Stories.

[1]An extent of land in which a *karīsa* (a dry measure) of seed can be sown, Sinhalese *kiriya* (often attested in ancient inscriptions).

INDEX

(In this Index persons or places with the same name are not always distinguished)

Abhaya 50
Abhibhū 53
Abhidhamma (Piṭaka) 104
Abodes, Pure 58
Accuta 127
advantages, ten 8, 13; twelve 8, 11
æon(s) 34, 39, 43, 46, 47, 48, 49, 50, 51, 52, 53, 54, 56, 57
Aggidatta 55
Ajapāla Banyan (tree) 20, 104, 108
Ajita 45
Akitti 58
Āḷāra (Kālāma) 89, 108
Alīnasattu 58
alms village 11
Amara 4, 8
Amaranth, Red 51
Amaravatī 3, 4
Amitā 48
Amity 105
Amity, Perfection of 30, 61
ammaṇa(s) 43, 83
analytical knowledge 36
Ānanda 20, 39, 48
Anāthapiṇḍika 103, 124, 125, 126, 127
Aṅga 117
Aññākoṇḍañña 110
anoja (flowers) 12
Anoma 45, 46, 50
Anomadassī 46, 47, 56
Anomā 47, 85, 86
Anotatta 67, 107
antecedents, causal 99
Anujā 56
Anupama 54
Anupiya 87
Anuruddha 38
Apaṇṇaka 1
apertures, nine 7
Arahant(s) 14, 16, 36, 37, 48, 110, 111, 114, 119
Arahantship 39, 74, 110, 111, 115, 122
Araka 59
Aratī 105
Arindama 53
Arjuna (tree) 46
arts, skill in 78
Aruṇa 53
Aruṇavatī 53
Āsāḷha 67, 85, 110
Āsāḷhi 66, 85, 109
Asama 45, 47
Asamā 47, 48
asaṅkheyya(s) 3, 4, 19, 20, 34, 43, 46, 57, 103, 104
ascetic(s), matted-hair 37, 111
aspiration(s) 20, 21, 103
Asoka 53
Asokā 44
Assaji 110, 114
Assattha (tree) 20, 21
assembly, fourfold 52
assurance(s) 35, 56, 57, 64, 89, 108
Asuras 88
Atideva 45
attachment(s) 6, 7, 10, 11, 13, 20, 21, 26, 56, 59, 81, 103, 106
attainments, eight 8, 10, 13, 14, 19, 36, 38, 43, 47, 72, 89
attendant virtues, twelve 8
Atthadassī 1, 49, 50, 56
attributes, ten 113
Atula 44, 53
austerities 89
Avīci 57, 94
Ayoghara 59

bag of flour-cake 59
Bamboo, Giant 49
Bamboo Grove 114, 115
Bandhumatī 53
Bandhumā 53
bane(s) 16, 17, 20, 21, 37, 117, 126
bane-free 36
Banyan (tree) 20, 56, 90, 92
Bārāṇasī 56, 108, 109, 116
bark garment, red 12
becoming, cycle of 57; three modes of 18
Bedchamber, Fragrant 125
Being, Great see Great Being
beings, departed 57
Bhadda 38
Bhaddā 45
Bhaddasāla 47
Bhaddavaggiya(s) 110
Bhaddiya 110
Bhalluka 107
Bhāradvāja 56
Bhāvitatta 44
Bhīyasa 55
Bhoja 74
Bhūridatta 58
Bilva (tree) 12
Bimbijāla (tree) 51
Bimbisāra 111
Bodhi (tree) 2, 19, 20, 25, 37, 38, 44, 45, 46, 47, 48, 49, 50, 51, 52, 53, 54, 55, 56, 71, 72, 93, 94, 95, 99, 103, 104, 109, 124
Bodhi (ascetic) 59
Bodhi-seat 99
Bodhisatta(s) 21, 22, 24, 25, 31, 33, 34, 38, 39, 40, 41, 42, 43, 45, 46, 47, 48, 49, 50, 51, 52, 53, 54, 55, 56, 57, 63, 64, 67, 68, 69, 70, 71, 72, 73, 74, 75, 76, 77, 78, 79, 80, 81, 82, 83, 84, 85, 86, 87, 88, 89, 90, 91, 92, 93, 94, 96, 97, 98, 116
Bodhisatta's Mother 69
boon 124
Brahmā(s) 63, 64, 70, 99, 100, 108, 109, 110, 123; world 38, 43, 95, 99
Brahmadatta 56
Brahmadeva 45, 52
Brahmā Sahampati 108
Brāhmaṇa family 65
brahmanical lore 3
Brotherhood (of monks) 35, 38, 41, 45, 46, 47, 48, 49, 53, 54, 55, 114, 124, 126
Buddha(s) 12, 14–36, 38–41, 43–57, 63, 64, 65, 66, 68, 72, 73, 75, 76, 79, 83, 84, 86, 88, 89, 91, 93, 94, 99, 100, 108, 109, 112, 113, 114, 118, 119, 120, 121, 124, 125, 126, 127
Buddhahood 18, 19, 64, 76
Buddha period 87
Buddha seedling 21
Buddha splendour 72
Buddha-to-be 73
Buddhadeva 2
Buddhahood 18, 19, 64, 76
Buddhamitta 1
Buddhavagga 106
Buddhavaṃsa 3, 4, 35
Buddhija 55

Cālā 52
camarī 26
campaka (flowers) 17
Campaka (city) 47
Campaka (tree) 50
Campakā 55
Campeyya 58
Canda 58
Candā 50, 53
Candakinnara Jātaka 123
Candamittā 53
Candavatī 46
canker-free 119
canker-waned 21
Cariyāpiṭaka 61
causal antecedents 99
causal origins 99
causes, phenomena which proceed from 114
Cetiyagiri 10
Chaddanta 58
chank (shell) 83
Channa 71, 82, 83, 84, 86, 87
characteristics, 75; major and minor 112; thirty-two 89, 90; threefold 64

China silk 55
Citralatā 69
city of the Devas 88
city of Tusita 61, 63, 66, 69
cloister(s) 8–12, 40, 89, 104, 125,
conch-shell 95
conditions, contributory 25–31, 57; four 97; eight 18, 57
congregation(s) 36
conversion 36
cosmic order 25
Crest Gem, Shrine of 86
cubit(s) 37, 38, 39, 44, 45, 46, 47, 48, 49, 50, 51, 52, 53, 54, 55, 56, 83, 84, 93, 94, 95
Cūlasubhaddā 125
Cūlasutasoma Jātaka 59
Cūḷāmaṇi (shrine) 86

Dāmā 54
Deer Park 108
deerskin with hooves 12
defects, five 8, 10
defilements 45, 64, 81
deities 32, 33, 34, 35, 41, 42, 43, 50, 51, 63, 64, 66, 71, 72, 78, 79, 83, 85, 89, 93, 95
Deities, Guardian 64, 67, 70, 91, 107
deity 84, 87, 91, 95
delusion 23, 87, 106
descent, pure 3
Deva (disciple) 49
Devadaha 69
Devala 48
devaputta 80, 95, 96
devas 36
Devas, city of 88
deva world 50
Dhaja 74
Dhamma 14, 15, 17, 18, 37, 40, 44, 72, 104, 108, 113, 115, 116, 126
Dhammā 50
Dhammadassī 49, 50, 51, 56
Dhammadinnā 50
Dhammaka (peak) 8, 9
Dhammapada 106
Dhammasena 44, 52
Dhanañjaya 58
Dhanapālaka 87
Dhanavatī 56
Dhaññavatī 45, 47
Dīgha, reciters of 79
Dīpa (tree) 37
Dīpappasādaka Mahinda 10
Dīpaṅkara 2, 14, 15, 16, 17, 19, 20, 21, 22, 24, 33, 34, 35, 36, 37, 38, 56, 57, 61, 121
directions, four 107; ten 25, 70
disadvantages, eight 8, 12, 13; nine 8, 11
disciples, chief 20, 37, 38, 44–56, 65, 115, 122
Discourse of the Proclamation of the Wheel of the Dhamma 109
Discourse on the Characteristics of Egolessness 110
Discourse on the Parable of Fire 111
discus 97
disc weapon 97
Dispensation 21, 22, 36, 37, 56, 75, 114
divine eye 86, 99, 108
divine vision 41
divinity 80
Doctrine 35, 36, 38, 39, 49, 52
dream, Māyā's 66
dreams, five great 91
Dumb Cripple 60

ecstatic utterance 103
Effort 105
Effort, Perfection of 27, 28, 60
Egolessness, Discourse on 110
eight advantages 10
eight attainments 8, 38, 72
eight attendant advantages 8
eight conditions 18, 57
eight disadvantages 12, 13
eight good qualities 10
eight handfuls 21
eight noble attainments 36
eight qualities 19
eight requisites 87
eight shortcomings 8, 12
eightfold attainments 19, 47
eighty minor marks 16, 120

Ekarāja 61
elephant, lordly white 67
emancipation 103, 104, 106, 107
empire, wheel of 84
Enlightened One(s) 34, 47, 48, 53, 54, 55, 56, 57, 63, 106, 109
Enlightenment 19, 20, 25, 26, 27, 28, 29, 30, 31, 32, 33, 34, 50, 57, 58, 74, 75, 78, 83, 88, 89, 90, 91, 92, 93, 94, 98, 109, 116, 124, 127
Enlightenment, tree of 21
Equanimity 105
Equanimity, Perfection of 31, 61
exertion(s) 8, 13, 16, 20, 27, 75, 87, 89, 90
existence, three states of 82
existences, knowledge of previous 99

Fig tree 55
Fire, Discourse on 111
fire, threefold 5, 81
fire sacrifice 111
Five, Group of 75, 76, 90, 108, 109
five defects 8, 10
five forms of higher knowledge 8
five great considerations 64
five great dreams 91
five great sacrifices 97
five kinds of flowers 74
five moral vows 66
five wishes 112
fivefold considerations 66
fivefold insight 19
fivefold intuitive knowledge 37, 38, 47
fivefold orchestra 42
flowers, five kinds of 74
force, resultant 40, 41
formula, twofold 108
four continents 65, 76
four deities 69
four directions 107
four great continents 49, 84
four Guardian Deities 107
four kinds of perfumes 74
Four Noble Truths 112
four omens 14, 76, 78, 79
four quarters 10
four spheres 26
fourfold analytical knowledge 39
fourfold assembly 52
fourfold fruits 36
Fragrant Bed-chamber 125
Fruit of Arahantship 110, 116
Fruit of the Non-Returner (Stage) 122, 124
Fruit of the Once-Returner (Stage) 122
Fruit of the Stream-Entrant (Stage) 110, 112, 114, 121, 122, 124
Fruits 93, 107

Gabled Hall 103
gandhabbas 22
Gavapāna 43
Gayāsīsa 111
Gaṇḍamba 104, 119
gāvuta(s) 72, 76, 79, 93, 112, 127
Generosity, Perfection of 25, 57, 58, 104
Ghaṭīkāra (Brahmā) 87, 92
Ghaṭīkāra (potter) 56
Giant Bamboo (tree) 49
Girimekhala 95, 97, 98
Golden Mountain 44
Gotama 19, 20, 32, 33, 43, 89, 109
Great Being 40, 41, 42, 43, 44, 64, 65, 66, 70, 75, 80, 85, 88, 89, 90, 92, 93, 94, 95, 96, 97, 98, 99, 120
Great Brahmā(s) 64, 70, 71, 87, 91, 92, 95, 108
Great Kadamba 48
Great Monastery 2, 114
Great Parinibbāna 127
Great Recluse 105, 111
Great Renunciation 20, 75, 80, 82, 83, 87
Great Sage 99
Great Soṇa 47
Group of Five 75, 76, 90, 108, 109
Guardian Deities 64, 67, 70, 91

hair relics 108
Haṃsavatī 48
Hare, the Wise 58
hatred 23, 31, 81, 84
Hatthipāla 59
Healing Star (Venus) 29
hermit, requisites of 10, 11
Himalayan 9

Himalayas 8, 11, 34, 67, 74
House of Gems, Shrine of 104

ill 64
impediment (*rāhula*) 81
impermanence 10
inheritance, Rāhula's 123
inheritance, transcendental 124
insight 19, 58, 99, 100, 109, 126; power of 8; fivefold 19
introspection, powers of 10
intuitive knowledge 13, 14, 16, 17, 22, 36, 37, 38, 43, 47, 51, 119
intuitive wisdom 10
Invitation 110
Ironwood (tree) 17, 44, 45
Isipatana 90, 109, 116

Jāli 103
Jambu tree 90
Jambudīpa 65, 114
Janapadakalyāṇī 123
Janasandha 52
Jātaka 1
Jātaka Commentary 83
Jaṭila 47, 48
Jayaddisa 59
Jayasena 51, 52
Jetavana (= Jeta's Grove) 103, 125, 126
Jewelled Cloister, Shrine of 104
jhāna(s) 14, 22, 38, 77, 89, 93, 107, 119
jhānic 46
Jitamitta 47
Jotipāla 56
joy, fivefold 42

Kadamba 48
kahāpaṇa(s) 3, 43, 127
Kajaṅgala 65
Kakusandha 54, 55, 56, 127
Kāla 93, 95
Kāḷadevala 71,72, 90, 119
Kāḷudāyī 115, 116, 117, 118
Kaṇhājinā 103
Kaṇikāra (flower) 51
Kanthaka 71, 82, 83, 84, 85, 86, 87
Kapila 20, 123
Kapilavatthu 20, 65, 66, 69, 72, 117, 120
Kappāsiya 110
karīsa 127
Kāsi 52, 60
kasiṇa 10
kasiṇa meditation 42
Kasi silk 55
Kassapa 49, 54, 56, 57, 111, 112, 121, 127
Kassapa Buddha 87
Ketaka (tree) 17
Khantivāda Jātaka 60
Kharadāṭhika 39, 40
Khattiya 37, 38, 44, 45, 47, 48, 52, 53, 65, 76, 81,121
Khaṇḍa 53
Khema 44, 52, 54, 55
Khemā 20, 51
Khemaṅkara 53
Kiṃsuka (tree) 96
King Suddhodana 115
Kisāgotamī 81
knowledge 97, 105
knowledge, analytical 36, 39
knowledge, higher 8, 10, 18, 57
knowledge, introspective 10
knowledge, intuitive 13, 14, 16, 17, 22, 36, 37, 38, 43, 47, 51, 119
knowledge, omniscient 99
knowledge of causal origins 99
knowledge of enlightenment 34
knowledge of omniscience 100
knowledge of past existences 99
knowledge, seat of 20
Kolita 20
Koṇāgamana 54, 55, 56, 127
Koṇḍañña 38, 44, 56, 74, 75, 89, 121
Kuddāla 59
Kutumbaka (flower) 80
Kuyyaka (flower) 80

lāja 67, 74
Lakkhaṇa 74
Laṭṭhivana 111, 112, 114
lay disciple by twofold formula 108
lion, Bodhisatta born as 46
lion's roar 24, 46, 71
Lokabyūha 63

Lokantarika 57
Lomahaṃsa 61
Lord of Ten Powers 113, 114
lordly white elephant 67
lore, brahmanical 3
Lumbinī Grove, Park 69, 71
lust 5, 84, 106

Maddī 103
Magadha 112, 117
Māgadhas 80
Mahādhammapāla 122, 124
Mahāgovinda 58, 59
Mahājanaka Jātaka 60
Mahākāla 95
Mahāmāyā 66, 69
Mahāmoggallāna 114
Mahānāma 110
Mahānāradakassapa Jātaka 112
Mahāpadāna 78
Mahāsāla 65
Mahāsammata 121
Mahāsubhaddā 125
Mahāsudassana 58
Mahāsutasoma 60
Mahāvana 103
Mahiṃsāsaka 2
Mahinda 10
Mahosadha 59, 71
Makhilā 53
Maṇḍa æon 49, 50, 51, 52, 54
Mandārava (flowers) 50, 52, 85
Maṅgala 38, 39, 44, 51, 56
mango grove 87
Mañjerika 95
Mantī 74
mantras 4
Māra 64, 84, 95, 96, 97, 98, 99, 104, 105, 106
marks, characteristic 73
marks, eighty minor 16, 120
marks, thirty-two major 16, 120
material substratum 74
matted-hair ascetic(s) 37, 111
Māyā 20 66
Medhaṅkara 56
meditation 9, 46, 93, 94, 107, 125
meditation, ecstatic 14, 77
meditation, *kasiṇa* 10, 42
meditation on cessation 46
meditation, seat of 94
mendicant 8, 12, 13, 19, 27, 75, 76, 77, 81, 86, 87, 88, 89, 109, 114
Meru (peak) 32
Middle Country 65, 107
milk rice 20, 67, 74, 91, 92, 93, 107
miracle(s) 72, 90, 91, 111, 118, 119, 120
miracle (of the double) 103, 104, 105, 119
miracle (of the shadow) 77
Moggallāna 114
Monarch, Universal 38, 49, 63, 64, 65, 68, 75
monasteries, advantages of donating 126
monastery, festival of dedication of 126
Morality, Perfection of 25, 26, 52, 58, 59
mother of Rāhula 78, 81, 120
Mucalinda 106, 107
Mūgapakkha Jātaka 60
muñja grass 11
musical instruments 68, 82, 85
Myrobalan (fruit) 52, 107

nāga(s) 18, 22, 32, 44, 53, 58, 85, 88, 93, 95, 98, 99, 107
Nāgā 49
Nāgalatā 107
Nāgasamālā 49
nahuta(s) 32, 111, 112
Nakulā 45
Nālaka 73
Nālaka Discourse 74
Nanda 123
Nandā 37
Nandana (Gardens) 66
Nārada (peak) 36
Nārada (Buddha) 46, 47, 48, 49, 56
Narasīha Gāthā 121
Nerañjarā 20, 92
Nibbāna 5, 6, 7, 17, 18, 35, 37, 44, 57, 74, 81, 91
Nigrodha (Grove) 118, 119
Nimi 58
nine apertures 7
nine disadvantages 11

ninefold faults 8
Nīpa (tree) 17
Nisabha 46
Noble Truths, four 112
noble states, ten 113
non-becoming 5
non-ego 64
Non-Returner 110

omens, four 14, 76, 78, 79
Omniscience 18, 60, 64, 75, 90, 99, 101, 104
omniscient knowledge 99
orchestra, fivefold 42
order, cosmic 25
ordination 36, 49, 57, 114, 123, 124
origins, interdependent causal 99
Osadha-dāraka 71

Pabbajjā Sutta 88
Pabbata 55
Pabhāvatī 49, 53
Pacceka Buddhas 65
Paduma 46, 47, 51, 56
Padumuttara 47, 48, 49, 56
Padumā 52, 53
palaces, three 77
Pālita 44, 50
palmyra fruit 93
Pañcavaggiya(s) 75, 76, 90, 108, 109
Paṇḍava 88
Paranimmita-vasavatti 64
Pāricchattaka (flowers) 52, 85
Pāṭali (tree) 53
Path(s) 93, 107, 110, 111
Patience 105
Patience, Perfection of 28, 60
Pāṭikaputta 104
Perfect Enlightenment 115
Perfect Emancipation 106
Perfections 31
Perfection of Amity 30, 61
Perfection of Effort 27, 28, 60
Perfection of Equanimity 31, 61
Perfection of Generosity 25, 57, 58, 104
Perfection of Morality 25, 26, 52, 58, 59, 105
Perfection of Patience 28, 60
Perfection of Renunciation 26, 59
Perfection of Resolution 29, 30, 60, 61
Perfection of Truth 29, 60
Perfection of Wisdom 27, 59, 60
Perfections 21, 32, 33, 34, 58, 61, 66, 96, 98, 104
Perfectly Enlightened One 108
perfumes, four kinds of 74
periods, three 2
Phagguṇa 116
Phagguṇī 47
Phussa 51, 52, 53, 56, 116
Phussā 52
Phussadeva 51
Pipphalī (tree) 37
Piyadassī 49, 50, 56
Piyaṅgu (tree) 50
Piṭakas, the three 52
portents, thirty-two 68, 71
powers, ten 113, 115, 116, 117, 125, 126
precepts 35, 49
precious things, seven 4
Proclamation of the Wheel of the Dhamma 109
Proclamation of Victory 98
proclamations, three tumultuous 63
psychic power 38
Punabbasumitta 126
Puṇḍarīka (tree) 54
Puṇṇā 91
punnāga (flowers) 12, 17
Pure Abodes 58
pure descent 3

qualities, eight 19
Queen Māyā 66

Ragā 105
Rāhu 35
rāhula (impediment) 81
Rāhula 81, 83, 122, 123, 124
Rāhula's Mother 71, 83, 122
Rāhula's Ordination 123
Rains' Retreat 110
Rājagaha 87, 111, 112, 113, 114, 115, 116, 117, 124, 125

Rājāyatana (tree) 107
Rāma 74
Rāmā 47, 48
Ramma 14, 17, 32, 33, 35
Rammaka 14
Rammavatī 37, 38
Reciters of the Dīgha (Nikāya) 79
Red Amaranth 51
red bark garment 12
Refuges 35, 44, 45, 48, 49, 112
Renunciation 58, 79, 87, 88, 105
Renunciation, Perfection of 26, 59
requisites of a hermit 10, 11
requisites of a monk 87
resolute will 18 57
Resolution 105
Resolution, Perfection of 29, 30, 60, 61
resultant force 40, 41
Retreat, Rains' 110
Revata 38, 45, 51, 56
Rose-apple (tree) 51, 77, 119
Rough Fangs 40

Sabbadassī 50
Sabbakāma 48
Sabbamitta 56
Sabbanāmā 51
Sabhiya 52
Sāgara 48, 50
Sāgata 37
Sahajātas (of simultaneous appearance), seven 72
Sahampati, Brahmā 108
Sākiya(s) 118, 119
Sakka(s) 8, 11, 41, 42, 43, 50, 64, 71, 80, 82, 86, 91, 95, 107, 108, 113, 114
Sakka's throne, heating of 41, 42, 80, 113
Sākyan 118
Sāla 32, 37, 47, 48, 67, 69, 93
Sāla grove 69
Sāla tree(s) 54, 69, 70
Sālakalyāṇi (tree) 38
saḷala 17
Saḷalavatī 65
sāli-rice 88
Salvation 1, 64
Sāma 80
Sāmā 55
Samālā 54
Sambahula 51
Sambhava 45, 52, 53
Saṃsāra 18, 58, 100, 103, 124
Samuddā 55
Saṅgha 113
Sañjaya 114
Sañjīva 55
Saṅkha 58
Saṅkhapāla Jātaka 59
Santa 50
Santusita(s) 64, 108
Sarabhaṅga Jātaka 78
Saraṇa 44, 48, 51
Saraṇaṅkara 56
Sāriputta 9, 11, 114, 115, 124
Sasa Jātaka 58
Sattubhasta Jātaka 59
Sāvatthi 103, 124, 125
School of Abhidhamma 104
seat of enlightenment 94
seat of knowledge 20
seat of meditation 94
Senaka 59
Senāni 90
service 19, 108, 110
sesamum 89
Setakaṇṇika 65
seven precious things 4
seven Sahajātas 71
seven strides 70
seven treasures 49
sevenfold noble treasure 124
shortcomings, eight 8, 12
Shrine of the Crest-gem 86
Shrine of the House of Gems 104
Shrine of the Jewelled Cloister 104
Shrine of the Steadfast Gaze 103, 104
Siddhattha 51, 52, 56, 75, 78, 80, 81, 88, 95, 96, 97, 98, 99, 103, 119, 120
Sikhī 53, 54, 56
Sīlavā 58
Sindhu breed 78
Sineru 63
Sirimā 44, 52
Sirīsa (tree) 55

Sītavana 124
Sīvalī 44, 51
Sivi 43, 58
six Vedaṅgas 74
six-coloured mass 16
sixfold intuitive knowledge 36, 37
Snowy Mountain 8
Sobhavatī 55
Sobhita 38, 45, 46, 50, 56
Somanassa 59
Soṇa (disciple) 54
Soṇa (tree) 47
Soṇā 44
sorrow 10, 31, 87
Sotthiya 55, 93, 127
Steadfast Gaze, Shrine of 103, 104
Steadfast Sage 99
Stream Entrant (stage) 110
striving 19, 75, 89, 122
Sub-Perfections 32, 97
Subhadda 38
Subhaddā 45
substratum, material 74
Sudassana (monastery) 14, 15
Sudassana (promontory) 36
Sudassana (city) 48
Sudassana (disciple) 49
Sudassana (king) 54
Sudassanā 50
Sudatta 44, 48, 74
Sudattā 48, 52
Sudda 65
Suddhodana 20, 65, 69, 72, 73, 75, 81, 89, 95, 115, 117
Sudeva 44, 47
Sudhamma (city) 45
Sudhamma (king) 45
Sudhammā 45, 50
Sudinna 50
Sugata 106, 108
Sujāta 48, 49, 50, 51, 52, 56
Sujātā 38, 45, 48, 50, 90, 91, 92, 107
Sumana 38, 44, 45, 48, 56
Sumanā 46
Sumaṅgala 37, 49, 127
Sumedha 3, 5, 7, 8, 9, 11, 14, 15, 16, 19, 21, 25, 26, 27, 28, 29, 30, 31, 33, 34, 35, 37, 48, 49, 56
Sumedhā 37
Sumitta 51
Sunanda 38
Sunandā 37, 51
Sundarī 46
Sunetta 45, 51
Sunimmita-vasavattis 108
supaṇṇa(s) 18, 85, 88, 93, 99
Suphassā 51
Suppatīta 54
Supreme Perfection(s) 32, 58, 59, 60, 61, 97
Supreme Perfection of Truth 60
Surakkhita 52
Surāmā 47, 48, 51
Suruci 41
Susīma 50
Sūtas 80
Suyāma(s) 64, 71, 74, 108

Tambapaṇṇi 114
Taṇhā 105
Taṇhaṅkara 56
Tapassu 107
Tathāgata(s) 15, 17, 20, 33, 35, 46, 51, 52, 74, 106, 107, 109, 111, 112, 115, 118, 125
Tāvatiṃsa 72, 86, 87
Teacher(s) 6, 14, 18, 32, 35–39, 41, 43–52, 54–57, 81, 103, 104, 106, 107, 108, 110–18, 120, 124, 125, 126
Teaching 37
ten advantages 8, 13
ten attributes 113
ten directions 25, 70
ten Noble States 113
ten Perfections 31, 32, 33, 34, 64, 96, 97, 105
ten Phenomena 113
ten Powers 14, 15, 16, 17, 21, 24, 56, 113, 115, 116, 117, 125, 126
ten Sub-perfections 32
ten Supreme Perfections 32
ten thousand fires in hell 23

ten thousand world spheres 21, 24, 44, 64, 68, 95, 100
ten thousand world systems 22, 33, 39, 44, 68, 84, 93, 99, 100
ten thousand worlds 22, 23, 35, 99
Terminalia Arjuna 46
thirty-two omens 68
thirty-two portents 68, 71
thirty-two characteristics 89, 90
thirty-two distinct marks 120
thirty-two marks 16
thousand world spheres 34
thousand-eyed Sakka 86
thousandfold world 22
thousands of world spheres 70
three Gems 114
three Fruits 124
three modes of becoming 18
three palaces 77
three periods 2
three Piṭakas 38, 56
three robes 87
three seasons 77
three tumultuous proclamations 63, 64
three Vedas 4, 49, 56, 74
three wisdoms 36
threefold uproar 63
threefold characteristics 64
Thūna 65
Tissa 37, 51, 52, 53, 56
Tissā 38
Tomentosa (tree) 52
tranquillity 9, 13
transiency 64
treasure, sevenfold noble 124
treasures 123; seven 49
treasure-urns, four 71
tree of Enlightenment 21
Truth 105
Truth, Perfection of 29, 60
Tusita (heaven) 2, 61, 63, 64, 66, 69, 101
twelve advantages 11
twelve attendant virtues 8
twelve virtues 11
twofold formula 108

Udaya 52
Udāyī 116, 117
Uddaka 108
Uddaka Rāmaputta 89
Udena 44
Ugga 127
Uggata 49
Ukkala 107
Universal Monarch(s) 38, 49, 63, 64, 65, 68, 75
Universal Ruler 123
universe, ridge of 85 93 94 95 98
Upacālā 52
Upaka 109
Upasanta 50, 54
Upasāla 47
Upasoṇā 44
Upatissa 20
Upatissā 38
uposatha 67
Uppalavaṇṇā 20
Uruvela Kassapa 111, 112
Uruvelā 56, 75, 89, 90, 110, 111, 116
usabha(s) 86, 93
Uttara 44, 48, 54, 55
Uttarā 44, 47, 55
utterance, ecstatic 100, 103
utterance, inspired 82
utterance, victorious 71

Vaṅka Rock 40
Vaṇṇabhūmi 112
Vappa 110
Varuṇa 45, 46, 47
Vasavatti 84
Vāseṭṭha 47
Vasu 87
Vebhāra 48, 51
Vedas, three 4, 49, 56, 74
Vedaṅgas, six 74
Veḷuvana 114, 115
Venus, the "healing star" 29
Vesākha 90, 91
Vesāli 103
Vessa 65
Vessabhū 53, 54, 55, 56, 127
Vessantara 2, 39, 57, 58, 61, 71, 98, 120
Vidhura 55, 59

Vijayuttara 95
Vijitāvī 38, 52
Vinaya 65
Vipassī 53, 54, 56, 126
Vipula 45
Vipulā 45
virtues, twelve 11
Visākha 23
Visākhā 55
Visākhā's mansion 126
Visayha 58
Vissakamma 9, 10, 11, 80

water, two streams of 70
Wheel of the Dhamma 14, 15, 34, 72, 109, 115
wheel of empire 84
wheels on the feet 38, 111
will, resolute 18 57
wisdom 20, 59, 75, 97, 110, 122, 123
Wisdoms, three 36
Wisdom, Perfection of 27, 59, 60, 105
wisdom, higher 8, 10, 13
wisdom, intuitive 10
Wise Hare 58
World Array 63
world of Brahmā 38
World Spheres, ten thousand 21, 24, 44, 64, 68, 95, 100
World Systems, ten thousand 22, 33, 39, 44, 68, 84, 93, 99, 100
Worlds, ten thousand 22, 23, 35, 99
Worthy One(s) 87, 89, 93, 106, 109, 115

Yakkha(s) 39, 40, 46, 93
Yakkha General 46
Yaññadatta 55
Yasa 110
Yasavā 46
Yasavatī 54
Yasodharā 46
yojana(s) 32, 36, 41, 42, 43, 48, 50, 53, 54, 65, 67, 72, 76, 79, 85, 86, 87, 90, 93, 95, 96, 98, 100, 109, 115, 117, 125, 127
Yugandhara 85